WEDDING
INSPIRATIONS

Margaret Caselton

text by Antonia Swinson

WEDDING
INSPIRATIONS

stylish ways to create a perfect day

RYLAND
PETERS
& SMALL
LONDON NEW YORK

photography by Polly Wreford

To my dear friend Sandy Boler, _MC_

Senior designer Catherine Griffin
Senior editor Annabel Morgan
Location research Claire Hector
Production manager Patricia Harrington
Art director Gabriella Le Grazie
Publishing director Alison Starling

Stylist Margaret Caselton
Text Antonia Swinson

First published in the United States in 2005 by Ryland Peters & Small, Inc
519 Broadway, 5th Floor
New York, NY 10012
www.rylandpeters.com

10 9 8 7 6 5 4 3 2 1

Text, design, and photographs © Ryland Peters & Small, Inc 2005

Printed and bound in China

Library of Congress Cataloging-in-Publication Data

Caselton, Margaret.
  Wedding inspirations : stylish ways to create a perfect day / Margaret Caselton ; text by Antonia Swinson ; photography by Polly Wreford.
    p. cm.
  ISBN 1-84172-792-X
  1. Weddings–Planning. 2. Weddings–Equipment and supplies. I. Swinson, Antonia. II. Title.
  HQ745C396 2005
  395.2'2–dc22
                                    2004018884

contents

THIS PAGE: *An idyllic scene awaits guests: a loggia overlooking a country garden is the backdrop for white tables set with colorful flowers, fine crystal, and floral china.*

I love weddings. They are such an affirmation of hope for the future. They are also the perfect opportunity for friends and family to celebrate the joy and happiness of the couple. And at the reception, the bride and groom can express their gratitude and affection by giving their guests a party to remember.

This book is for everybody who has a wedding to look forward to. It is a book of ideas for you to adapt to suit your own particular style and theme. The book begins with a chapter on planning, to point you in the right direction. Next follows sections on different wedding styles to demonstrate how to combine decorative elements to produce a finished look that's coordinated and stylish, but still personal. Chapters on separate elements follow: bridal flowers and floral decorations; confetti; cakes; table settings; favors; and candles. Attention to detail makes all the difference, and it's often the little things that create the biggest impression.

The book is designed to inspire, so pick and mix the things that suit you and your wedding. It's a compliment to everyone who attends your wedding to make the day as beautiful as it can be. Most importantly, have fun, both during the planning and, above all, on the day!

Margaret Caselton

a day to remember…

FAR LEFT: *Delicate floral detail on the china reinforces a color scheme of soft pinks and plums.*
LEFT: *A diaphanous purple ribbon tied into a large bow around a wineglass stem is a simple but striking touch.*
ABOVE: *A table centerpiece contrasts white stephanotis with ruby red carnations, making a dramatic and sophisticated statement.*

planning

PLANNING A WEDDING IS AN EXCITING BUT INTIMIDATING
PROSPECT, SO GOOD ORGANIZATION IS ABSOLUTELY VITAL.
ONCE YOU'VE SET THE DATE, BEGIN BY COLLECTING
ANYTHING THAT INSPIRES YOU, THEN START TURNING
YOUR DREAMS INTO REALITY...

GATHERING INSPIRATION

Organizing a wedding involves many decisions and lots of elements—the dress, flowers, cake, food, decorations, and so on. Having a clear sense of what you want to achieve before you start is the best way to avoid a result that looks ill-conceived or thrown together. So time spent planning is never wasted time. Putting in the thought and groundwork months before the big day is essential if you want your vision to become reality.

This doesn't mean that stylish weddings must be elaborate and expensive. Far from it. If yours is an informal country wedding, jam jars overflowing with

wild flowers would be fabulous table centerpieces. However, even this look of rustic simplicity needs to be carefully followed through, right down to the last favor, if it is to be a success. Planning early allows you time to explore different options and shop around. It also gives you the chance to start again if something doesn't work out the way you wanted.

One of the best ways to get the ball rolling is to start collecting things that capture something of the look you're after. You might end up with pictures from magazines, scraps of fabric, paint charts, ribbons, flowers, even inspirational words or phrases. Tack up a length of string along a wall or the side of a cupboard, and attach your objects to it. Then live with them for a week and see how the items work together, how well the colors complement each other, and

OPPOSITE AND ABOVE: *Putting up a piece of string and pegging objects to it, just as you would washing, is one way of building up a collection of items that inspire you and sum up the look you want to achieve at your wedding.*
RIGHT: *Another approach is to create a mood board, much in the way that fashion designers do, pinning up your sources of inspiration so that you can live with them and see how they work together before making any final decisions.*

whether a coherent picture is emerging. On similar lines, you could pin everything up to make a mood board. Either way, these visual aids are an easy and effective way to clarify your ideas and find out what works and what doesn't. Choosing a place to hold the reception will be an early, and crucial, decision. Make sure that the style you're striving for will sit easily in its surroundings. As our four styles of wedding show (see pages 14–29), working with a location, and never against it, is the way to achieve a beautiful result.

Finally, remember that regardless of how complicated organizing a wedding is, it should be a pleasure, not a burden. Enjoy planning the event of a lifetime and don't lose sight of what's at the heart of it all—the solemnization of a loving union and the celebration of a new chapter in your life.

OPPOSITE: *Before ordering your invitations, collect examples of paper, fonts, and inks. Your wedding stationery will be the first indication your guests receive of the type of day you're planning.*
ABOVE: *Suspension files are a good way of organizing your wedding paperwork. Make sure they're colorful rather than purely utilitarian, so that they remind you of fun rather than work.*
LEFT: *Attractive albums are another way of collecting ideas. Slip clippings, swatches, and pictures within their pages, and turn them into keepsakes after the wedding's over.*

LEFT: *The bride's ensemble is, like the setting, elegant, streamlined, and simple.* BELOW LEFT: *To display place cards unfussily in such a minimalist tablescape, they are tucked inside the wineglasses.* RIGHT: *Tall, tapered vases hold two towering stems of agapanthus in a display of Asian-inspired grace. Stainless-steel and glass candleholders add a softening note of warmth, but everything about the table setting is pared down and pure.*

MODERN WEDDING

A location as strikingly architectural and uncompromisingly modern as this one cries out for an equally minimalist style of reception. An all-white color scheme is the obvious choice, successfully combining simplicity with romance. For the table setting, white china has been partnered with plain silver cutlery, glass votives and vases, and etched glassware. Tradition has not been dispensed with altogether—there are white damask napkins and a three-tiered wedding cake—but the whole affair has been approached in a spirit of simplicity. Nor has nature been forgotten: there are flowers, shells, and an emphasis on circles and curves in the table setting. The white-on-white theme produces a serene look that is prevented from spilling over into the clinical by the spectacular view over the lake to the lush trees beyond.

The head table dominates the room, with chairs inspired by Arne Jacobsen's Series 7 neatly lined up down one side. When a table setting is as simple as this one, the elements need to be selected and arranged with great care. Here, even the chairs have been placed so that they form a perfectly straight line. Slender glass vases holding two agapanthus

THIS PAGE: *The head table is positioned to offer a view of the bridal couple set against a backdrop of water, trees, and sky. The color scheme is all white, and every element of the table setting has been laid out with exacting precision.*

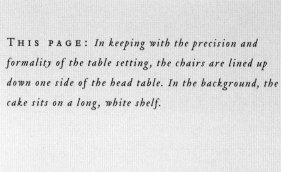

THIS PAGE: *In keeping with the precision and formality of the table setting, the chairs are lined up down one side of the head table. In the background, the cake sits on a long, white shelf.*

OPPOSITE, ABOVE: *Despite the austerity of the setting, there is softness here, too. Etched glasses and spiraling shells contribute a subtle theme of circles, while the napkins are thick, luxurious damask.*

stems are set at every third place setting, and the stainless-steel candleholders sit to the top left of each plate at even intervals. Such precision creates a rhythm and pattern that is responsible for the success of this look. In a sparsely set tablescape, it is also vital that the items used have an elegance and beauty of form. Here, a subtle theme of circles runs throughout, thanks to the etched glasses, grooved plates, and gleaming shells that sit on top of each napkin. The cake, too, nods to the circle motif, with its decoration of icing "pearls," graduating from large to small on each tier. Without these careful details, the table would be in danger of looking too austere. It is important that among sleek, hard-edged materials there are softening touches. The delicate blooms, flickering votives, and heart-shaped ice cubes in the chunky glass ice buckets all serve as reminders that this is, after all, a wedding.

Did you know THAT IN THE MIDDLE AGES A WHITE WEDDING CAKE WAS PRIZED NOT AS A SYMBOL OF THE BRIDE'S PURITY BUT OF HER FAMILY'S WEALTH? THE PURER AND WHITER THE SUGAR USED IN THE ICING, THE MORE EXPENSIVE THE CAKE.

RIGHT: *The wedding cake combines tradition and modernity. Its three tiers are decorated with ever-decreasing opalescent icing "pearls" and it is topped with a cluster of immaculate eucharis lilies.*
FAR RIGHT: *A champagne bottle sits chilling in a glass bucket filled with heart-shaped ice cubes.*

RIGHT: *A terrace provides the setting for the wedding reception, with views of the garden beyond providing the backdrop to the celebrations. A color scheme of blues and pinks against white gives the scene a summery prettiness.*

OPPOSITE, ABOVE LEFT: *Glasses with colored stems double up as place card holders, and fabric roses sit on the hand-decorated plates.*

OPPOSITE, ABOVE RIGHT: *The favors are concealed in pink boxes decorated with sheer ribbon and a fresh pink rosebud.*

Did you know THAT WHITE WEDDINGS WERE POPULARIZED BY THE VICTORIANS? BEFORE THEN, BRIDES WORE THEIR BEST DRESS, SOMETIMES WITH THE ADDITION OF A WHITE RIBBON TO SYMBOLIZE PURITY.

RELAXED WEDDING

Smaller wedding receptions are perfectly suited to more informal surroundings, making guests feel welcome, at ease, and at home. This setting is the terrace of a country house, where the scents, sights, and sounds of a summer garden can be enjoyed without worrying about bad weather. The emphasis is on color, with white acting as a foil for candy pink, baby blue, and accents of deep pink. Flowers are an important motif for this table setting, since the whole garden and its glorious flowers are the backdrop for the occasion.

A white linen tablecloth covers the table completely. Using a covering which reaches to the floor—whether it be a tablecloth, sheet, or length of fabric—produces a clean look, concealing distracting table legs. The napkins are in shades of palest pink and blue rather than the usual white, alternating around the table. Folding metal garden chairs have been smartened up with seat and back covers in a rose- and stripe-patterned fabric that picks out the day's key colors. Chinese-style paper lanterns hold votive candles and hang from a

garland of ivy swagged between the arches of the terrace. Lighting plays an important role in creating an intimate, romantic atmosphere, and outdoor string lights, flares stuck in the ground, or metal lanterns placed along a wall would all work well, casting a magical glow as the evening approaches.

On the tables, glasses with pastel-colored stems, to which name tags have been tied with narrow ribbon, continue the colorful theme. The white china has freehand circular patterns drawn into the glaze, and each plate is decorated with a lush fabric cabbage rose. Votives are placed inside cream-painted wire baskets, the open sides casting intricate shadows across the table. The favors have been packaged in two ways. Some sit on gilt-edged china, housed in magenta boxes tied with sheer ribbon and finished with a rose. Others, in white boxes with white ribbon, have been arranged on a cake stand that also displays the table number, creating a simple but striking centerpiece.

OPPOSITE, ABOVE LEFT: *Votive candles inside Chinese lanterns provide a romantic glow as day turns into evening.*
OPPOSITE, BELOW LEFT: *More favors, this time arranged on a cake stand, as a centerpiece for the table.*
OPPOSITE, RIGHT: *The seats and backs of folding metal garden chairs are dressed up with fabric covers.*
ABOVE LEFT: *Votives flicker inside cream-painted wire baskets.*
ABOVE RIGHT: *Pale pink and blue napkins are in keeping with the wedding's colorful theme.*

C L A S S I C   W E D D I N G

The classic wedding look is one governed by tradition and formality. It is a style that lends itself to grand locations, such as stately homes or hotels. Surroundings as majestic as this—a paneled room with lofty proportions and a spectacular chandelier—must be the starting point for your scheme. Take your cue from your venue's color scheme, then create a look in sympathy with it. Here, a white, cream, and gold theme was suggested by the wall color and the marble fireplace and gilded mirror. The fireplace dominates the room, forming a natural focal point that lends itself to decoration. The three-armed candelabra has been echoed by a candle still life in the empty grate. Large pillar candles of different heights form a magical display that creates a sense of welcome and celebration.

This is a rich, lavish scheme but not an overwhelming one, thanks to the exceptionally light and airy quality of the space. Flowers, used in extravagant abundance, play a key role. Roses, tulips, mimosa, snowberries, and ivy have

A B O V E   L E F T : *Large pillar candles bring a warm, romantic glow to the empty hearth, creating a sense of welcome. Various heights have been used to create the best effect when the candles are lit.*

A B O V E   R I G H T : *Open-backed gilt chairs are a popular choice for weddings. They look particularly pretty with flower arrangements cascading down the back.*

O P P O S I T E : *An imposing marble fireplace and ornate mirror dominate this room, offering a natural focal point and the ideal place for an extravagant floral garland.*

been used to create a magnificent garland across the fireplace, anchored by two floral clusters. The table arrangements sit in silver stands, while the chairs are decorated with cascades of flowers down their backs. The effect is soft and romantic.

A pristine white tablecloth sets the tone for the sumptuous table setting. The dinnerware is white with a gold rim, with one gold-striped plate to provide visual contrast. Gilt-edged glassware continues the theme. Gold dominates the table, right down to the ribbon adorning the chocolate favors. Contrasting accents of silver—in the form of flatware and flower stands—have been deliberately introduced to ensure that the effect doesn't become oppressively opulent. In the same way, gilt chairs with open backs have been used in preference to solid chairs. This is a look of great refinement and elegance, extravagant without being fussy, formal without being rigid.

Did you know THAT THE PRACTICE OF HOLDING A WEDDING RECEPTION HAS ITS ROOTS IN THE MEDIEVAL PERIOD? THE GROOM WAS SUPPOSED TO GIVE GIFTS OF FOOD AND DRINK TO HIS IN-LAWS IN ORDER TO DEMONSTRATE THAT HE COULD SUPPORT HIS NEW WIFE.

OPPOSITE AND LEFT: *The gold-and-white dinnerware and gold-rimmed glassware have a look of stately elegance. Bags of chocolate truffles, tied with gold ribbon, await the guests.*

FAR LEFT: *The floral centerpieces, arranged in a gently domed shape, sit in gleaming silver stands.*

ABOVE: *A floral swag decorates the majestic fireplace, held in place by two loose clusters of flowers that echo the table arrangements.*

LEFT: *A posy of flowers tied with green ribbon decorates the back of one of the chairs to mark the head of the table.*
OPPOSITE: *Weeping willows are a glorious backdrop for the pink, green, and white tables. Flowers are are the key motif, from the centerpieces to the patterned china and favors.*

ABOVE: *Country flowers such as lupines, roses, stock, and blackberries overflow from glass vases on the table.*
BELOW: *The bridesmaids' bouquets, composed of the same flowers, have been tied with a big bow of green satin ribbon.*

COUNTRY WEDDING

A summer garden is a reception setting of enormous charm and romance. You'll need to feel extremely confident of fine weather to risk an entirely alfresco celebration, so having a tent will probably form part of your plans. A rural location is very much a blank canvas, leaving you free to decide whether you want the reception to be a formal affair or a laidback occasion, with children and pets running across the lawn. The mood here is relaxed, with the emphasis on cottage-garden flowers and a color scheme of pink and green, prompted by the verdant surroundings.

For the meal, simple banquet tables have been set end to end and covered with white cotton sheets to conceal the legs. Large damask tablecloths have been laid on top on the diagonal, to create a diamond shape. Collapsible garden chairs provide the seating, although for an informal at-home wedding, a mix-and-match collection of garden benches and chairs from the house would

have its own charm. Tall glass vases, overflowing with lush flowers, provide a centerpiece. Roses, lupines, cow parsley, stock, and ripening blackberries have been used, all in tones of green and pink. To avoid an overly sugary look, rich pinky-reds have been introduced alongside the pastel shades. To mark the head of the table, a bouquet of flowers, tied with wide, green satin ribbon, has been attached to the chair back.

For the table setting, floral china has been chosen to continue the pink and green theme. As with the chairs, for a small wedding at home an assortment of different floral china could work well. A combination of glassware has been used—pale green glass, etched designs, and plainer, clear glasses. The whole table setting has been overlaid with a loose web of tiny, green glass hearts on fine wire. The favors, which also act as place cards, are a particularly pretty detail, consisting of small, white boxes decorated with narrow green ribbon and a fresh rose of the sort used in the table arrangements and bouquets.

the great outdoors

ABOVE LEFT: *Accents of deeper pinks give the flower arrangements depth. Sweet-smelling stock ensures the air is filled with summer perfume.*
ABOVE RIGHT: *Sunlight filters through the glasses, creating pools of color on the white cloth.*

LEFT AND ABOVE: *Banquet tables covered in white cotton sheets and white garden chairs help to set the tone for the reception, ensuring a relaxed and friendly atmosphere. The finished result is idyllic.*

flowers

FLOWERS AND WEDDINGS ARE A MATCH MADE IN HEAVEN.
NOTHING IS MORE ROMANTIC THAN FRESH FLOWERS,
WHETHER CASCADES OF ROSES OR RICHLY SCENTED LILIES.
SURROUNDING YOURSELF WITH FLOWERS WILL ENCHANT
THE SENSES AND LEAVE YOU WITH FRAGRANT MEMORIES.

BRIDAL FLOWERS

ABOVE: A hydrangea head has been sewn onto braid to create a wrist corsage. The green-tinged flowers and pink and green braid echo the wedding's color theme.

ABOVE CENTER: A slender sheaf of calla lilies is secured with a eucharis lily tucked into an organza bow, complementing the modern, clean lines of the bride's dress.

The tradition of the bridal bouquet began many centuries ago, with brides carrying posies of aromatic herbs to ward off evil spirits. But today a bridal bouquet is purely decorative, and designed to heighten the beauty of the wedding ensemble.

Traditionally, bouquets were wired, an intricate and time-consuming task that produces a stiff, formal look. The current vogue is for hand-tied bouquets, a technique that gives a looser, more relaxed result. A slender sheaf of flowers, such as lilies, carried in the crook of the arm, takes the style to its most sleek and modern. The more traditional approach is a fuller, rounder bouquet. Although it's usual for the bride to have a larger bouquet than the bridesmaids, there are no rules, so go with whatever suits your dress and makes you happy.

Collaborating with a professional florist is, for most brides, a new experience. For your first meeting with them, take along your treasure trove of inspirational objects (see Planning, pages 8–13), a picture of your dress, and a scrap of its fabric. All this will help your florist to get an idea of the style of wedding that you are trying to create.

THIS PAGE: *Single-variety bouquets have a simplicity about them that lets the beauty of the flowers shine through. This loose posy of exquisite eucharis lilies looks informal and yet luxurious.*
OPPOSITE, ABOVE RIGHT: *The blooms have such a strong form that only one is needed to make a striking headdress.*

Color is usually the first thing that brides discuss with their florist. White is the classic wedding choice, pure and elegant. There are few things more exquisite than a flawless bouquet of white roses or lilies. Pink is a feminine, romantic choice, particularly the paler, blushing tones, while it can create a bold effect at the deeper end of the spectrum. Blue flowers are cool and serene, and there are some good candidates if it's your favorite color: grape hyacinths in spring; cornflowers and delphiniums in summer; and hydrangeas in late summer and early autumn. Purples are dramatic at their darkest, and ethereal when they're shades of mauve and lilac. Yellow is cheerful and positive, while orange is richer and fiery. Red is the color of passion. The brightest reds are a good match for the intense light of a summer day, while cooler reds look wonderful in winter. Green is, of course, the color of foliage, but there are also green-tinged flowers which can be used to produce a fresh, tranquil look, such as lady's-mantle, viburnum, and cymbidium orchids.

Did you know THAT BOUQUETS BEGAN THEIR LIFE CENTURIES AGO AS POSIES OF AROMATIC HERBS, CARRIED BY THE BRIDE BECAUSE IT WAS THOUGHT THAT THEY HAD THE POWER TO WARD OFF EVIL SPIRITS?

OPPOSITE, ABOVE
LEFT, AND BELOW
LEFT: *Hair accessories*
for the bridesmaids have
been made by wiring fresh
flowers onto a hair elastic
and a headband.
OPPOSITE, BELOW
RIGHT: *The*
bridesmaids' flowers are
similar to the bride's
bouquet, but with some
accents of deeper color from
roses and ripening
blackberries.
LEFT: *High romance for*
high summer: this bouquet
is an unashamedly pretty
mixture of soft pinks and
white, and includes roses,
carnations, and scabiosa.

THIS PAGE: *Hydrangeas are wonderful for late summer and early autumn color, and are available in a range of pinks and blues, from very pale through to red and almost purple. The rounded softness of the many-petaled heads helps to create a very feminine, romantic look.*

pink perfection

Single-color bouquets are always popular, whether using exactly the same shade or a mixture of light and dark tones, but you might want a more eclectic approach. Colors which lie next to each other on the color wheel—such as yellow and orange, or purple and pink—produce harmonious partnerships. Colors that sit opposite each other, such as blue and orange, or red and green, create more vibrant effects. Using pale shades will tone down a combination, while darker ones will intensify it. If this sounds daunting, remember that it's a professional florist's job to know how to use color. As a starting point, browse around your local florists, seeing which flowers immediately appeal to you and how they look together.

You can then think about the flowers you want to use. Many of the best-loved flowers are available all year round, among them roses, tulips, carnations, orchids, and lilies. They all come in a wide range of colors and last well as cut flowers, and it's extremely useful for

THIS PAGE: *For this bridesmaid's bouquet, palest pink hydrangeas have been surrounded by their own lush green leaves and secured with pink satin ribbon. The bouquet matches the cake shown opposite (and on page 75).*

OPPOSITE: *This bouquet of silk roses in mellow pastel tones, tied with plum-colored ribbon, looks just as good as the real thing. Silk bouquets can be bought ready-made, or created with single stems in the same way as real bouquets.*

florists to have these stalwarts to rely on at any time of year. However, it's worth using seasonal flowers, since they'll be easily available and are often good value for money. In spring there are daffodils, tulips, ranunculuses, and anemones; in summer, sweet peas, cornflowers, peonies, and delphiniums. Autumn flowers include hydrangeas, chrysanthemums, New York asters, and many berries; winter offers amaryllis, hellebores, snowdrops, pansies, and camellias.

Although the appearance of flowers is all-important, don't forget that many of them smell as wonderful as they look. Although we all associate roses with glorious perfume, many of the varieties bred for the floristry trade are scentless. If it's a heady aroma that you want, let your florist know when you first meet. It may be that you will need to use garden varieties begged from generous family and friends. Other flowers at the top of the scent chart are lily of the valley, gardenias, stephanotis, sweet peas, and jasmine.

rich reds

ABOVE LEFT AND RIGHT: *Roses look wonderful used on their own because they create a dense, textured effect when they're tightly packed together. Dark, luscious, velvety red roses are a particularly effective choice for a winter wedding.*

LEFT AND BELOW: *Tulips are excellent value and available all year round in a huge range of colors. Massed together, they make for an exuberant bouquet. Here, the stems have been bound with wide wire-edged ribbon that is fastened in place with pearl-headed dressmaker's pins. Another length of ribbon has been wound around the stems and finished with a large bow.*

Did you know THAT IN THE LANGUAGE OF FLOWERS, ROSES SYMBOLIZE LOVE; LAVENDER, DEVOTION; VIOLETS, FAITHFULNESS; LILIES OF THE VALLEY, SWEETNESS AND PURITY; AND GYPSOPHILA, FRUITFUL MARRIAGE?

There are, of course, other ingredients that can be used in bouquets in combination with flowers. In winter, bare twigs or seed heads can look very striking. Sprays of wired beads add glamorous sparkle to a bouquet, as do feathers or wired sequined butterflies. You can mist spray paints over flowers (metallics are an obvious choice) and even coat them with glitter (both these techniques work particularly well on roses, which are robust enough to carry off such effects). For a soft, romantic look, envelop your bouquet in a cloud of white tulle.

Although the stem of a bouquet serves the very practical purpose of being there for the bride to hold onto, it can be used for decorative effect, too. One way to conceal the stem of a bouquet is to wrap it completely in thick ribbon, fixing the ribbon in place with pearl-headed dressmaker's pins. Alternatively, a bouquet can simply be hand-tied. Fashioning the ribbon into a large bow always looks pretty (wire-edged ribbon holds its shape well). You could also

RIGHT: *Using ribbon to tie
or bind a bouquet adds an extra
element of color and decoration.
The organza ribbon tying this
cluster of white roses links up
with other touches of blue used
throughout the wedding.*

use long lengths of ribbon in various harmonizing shades, and leave the ends
trailing like streamers. All these exquisite finishing touches help to heighten
the beauty of a bridal bouquet.

The style of your flowers is a natural extension of the rest of the wedding,
and you'll probably have set the tone of the day by the time you plan your
flowers. If the occasion is going to be chic and modern, you'll want flowers with
a striking, architectural quality, such as arum lilies or dendrobium orchids. For
a very formal wedding, you may want a structured bouquet with lots of classic
white wedding flowers, such as roses, stephanotis, and gardenias. For a

summer country wedding, a large, loose bunch of cottage-garden favorites such as sweet peas, lupines, and poppies would be perfect. If your wedding is fun and informal, a bouquet of sunflowers might appeal. You'll need to decide if you want a large, dramatic bouquet or something smaller and more compact, and whether you want a floral headdress. For little flower girls there are lots of possibilities, including garlands, decorated wreaths, floral balls, and flower-filled baskets. Whatever kind of arrangement you choose, it's vital that you feel comfortable carrying it, a consideration that's also important for young attendants, who'll soon tire of cumbersome bouquets.

Flowers are a potent symbol of love and celebration, and have played a part in wedding festivities for centuries—the Romans, for instance, sprinkled rose petals on the marriage bed. Whether you choose a magnificent armful of roses or a bunch of Queen Anne's lace tied with ribbon, enjoy their fleeting beauty, and savor their memory long after the day is over.

country chic

A BOVE AND BELOW RIGHT: *"Tails" of ribbon in shades of blue and white add a pretty touch to these informal, rustic bouquets for the bride and her attendants. The flowers used include roses, delphiniums, and lupines.*
R IGHT: *There's no reason why beloved pets shouldn't look their best on the big day, too.*
O PPOSITE: *A mixed bouquet of white garden flowers, including stock and roses, looks charming, delicate, and fresh, with crisp white ribbon binding the stems to continue the single-color theme.*

OPPOSITE AND THIS PAGE: *At a romantic country wedding, pure white is the predominant color, with accents of soft blue, pink, and green, a palette concocted from roses, stock, freesias, and snowberries. Floral headdresses, a ribbon sash decorated with roses, and posies with streaming ribbons, all add to the carefree effect. A decorated wicker wheelbarrow adds a touch of whimsy.*

BOUTONNIERES

It's traditional for the groom's boutonniere to take its cue from the bride's bouquet. There's no reason to follow the idea literally, of course, but it does add to the overall coherence of the flower scheme if the boutonnieres echo the composition of the bride's and bridesmaids' flowers.

It's usual for the groom, best man, the groomsmen, and both the bride's and groom's father to wear special boutonnieres, but there may be other men you'd like to extend the courtesy to, such as brothers, nephews, or grandfathers. You could even consider providing boutonnieres as favors for all your male guests, displayed on trays or in baskets in the entrance way to the wedding ceremony. If you do this, give one of the groomsmen the job of handing them out, and make sure you've got a plentiful supply of pins.

A single rose is the classic choice for a boutonniere and there are few things which look as elegant. However, there are plenty of other smart possibilities, from individual flowers to combining several blooms. Try a flawless single gardenia, tulip, or camellia, or narcissi, ranunculuses, lilies of the valley, or orchids. Foliage is important, too, and helps to frame the flowers.

Consider scent when choosing flowers for boutonnieres, since they are placed at just the right level to be smelled by the wearer. Hyacinth

OPPOSITE, ABOVE:
*This yellow and white
boutonniere of orchids,
white irises, and mimosa
has had its stem bound with
narrow ribbon in an
elegant crisscross pattern.*
OPPOSITE,
BELOW: *Boutonnieres
don't have to be uniform in
composition. Here, a
selection of complementary
arrangements is displayed
on an ornate tray, ready for
collection by male members
of the bridal party.*
LEFT: *Unusual
combinations can produce
charming results. Here,
rosebuds and heather (for
luck) partner each other,
their stems bound in
lustrous velvet ribbon.*

Did you know THAT THE TRADITION OF THE GROOM WEARING A FLOWER IN HIS JACKET LAPEL TAKEN FROM HIS BRIDE'S BOUQUET GOES BACK TO THE MEDIEVAL PERIOD, WHEN A KNIGHT WORE HIS LADY'S COLORS AS A LOVE TOKEN?

A B O V E A N D A B O V E R I G H T : *Roses make undeniably elegant boutonnieres. It's a nice idea for the groom's boutonniere to be distinct from the others. Here, his flawless rose is white, while the other men wear pinky-red blooms.*

florets, stephanotis, roses, sweet peas, jasmine, or stock (see picture opposite) would all be wonderfully fragrant. Alternatively, there are aromatic herbs such as rosemary and lavender.

Although a boutonniere is a flower arrangement in miniature, the stem can be wrapped for additional decoration in just the same way as a bouquet. Interesting ribbons and braids in seductive colors and textures can be fastened with dressmaker's pins in various ways. Ribbon can be tightly bound around the stem to cover it completely (see page 47); or it can be wrapped to create a spiral or crossover pattern up the length of the stem. If the ribbon is fine enough, it can be tied into a little bow under the head of the flowers.

A B O V E : *A trio of colorful boutonnieres. On the left, summery pink spray roses and rose leaves; in the middle, scented white stock and variegated ivy; on the right, a red rose and dark ivy leaf.*

DECORATIONS
& ARRANGEMENTS

Bouquets are usually a bride's first consideration when planning wedding
flowers. Once chosen, the bouquet will set the style for other flowers at the
wedding, on tables, chairs, and around the reception room. The color scheme
and key flowers usually take their cue from the bridal arrangements, but the
surroundings will also help to determine the look of the reception displays (see
the chapters on Modern, Relaxed, Classic, and Country weddings for more
pointers). The level of formality or informality is important. For a traditional,
grand reception, the flowers should have a similar quality. This may take the
form of very precisely placed arrangements, forming a rhythmic display on the

table. Formality may also express itself in the placing of the flowers themselves, as is shown by the artfully angled roses on this page. If the wedding is adopting a more relaxed mood, looser, fuller arrangements with a "just-picked" quality, spilling over the sides of their containers onto the table tops, may be the answer (see the garden wedding on pages 60–61).

Whatever style you adopt, one vital rule is to make sure that your table arrangements don't detract from the main business of the day, which is eating, drinking, talking, and having fun. Towering displays on table tops will only impede the flow of conversation. Guests should be able to see over or through arrangements easily and be able to reach items on the table such as glasses, salt shakers, or butter dishes. Don't forget that beautifully scented flowers on your tables (see page 53) will

OPPOSITE: *An abundance of white and green creates a soft, dreamy look. The centerpieces include calla lilies, lady's mantle, and viburnum. A eucharis lily lies on each napkin.*

LEFT AND ABOVE RIGHT: *Single white rosebuds have been stripped of their thorns and lower leaves to striking effect. Displayed in bud vases, they are beautifully simple yet romantic.*

ABOVE: *A shallow silver dish crammed with blowsy white roses makes for a luscious, low-level display that guests can easily talk over.*

Did you know THAT IN PAST CENTURIES, PEOPLE BELIEVED THAT TAKING PIECES OF THE BRIDE'S FLOWERS OR CLOTHES WOULD HELP THEM SHARE HER GOOD FORTUNE? TO ESCAPE GRABBING HANDS, THE BRIDE WOULD THROW HER BOUQUET AS SHE LEFT, THE ORIGIN OF TODAY'S TOSSING THE BOUQUET.

greatly enhance your guests' enjoyment of the reception. If you want something big and spectacular, place these arrangements around the reception room, perhaps standing in corners and alcoves or flanking fireplaces, where they can be appreciated while the meal is eaten.

The containers you use for your arrangements are as crucial to the success of the result as the flowers placed in them. Vases are available in a multitude of materials, sizes, and colors, but you can use almost anything to house flowers. Cake stands, bowls, pitchers, soup tureens, or serving dishes can all be used, or (particularly if you're having a small wedding) you might want to find your own containers from tag sales or thrift stores. There's no rule saying that containers have to match, but if you are going for an eclectic look, strive for one element of continuity—in terms of shape, color, or material—to

OPPOSITE: *For this pink- and white-themed wedding, hydrangeas are the key flower. China, cake, napkins, and flower arrangements await the guests, laid out on a long table garlanded with ivy and eucharis lilies. A cylindrical vase holds a cluster of frothy hydrangeas, which also form the bridesmaids' bouquets (see page 36) and decorate the cake (see page 75).*

LEFT AND ABOVE: *The delights of a scented garden have been brought indoors for this reception. Pots of lily of the valley act as favors and place markers, while table numbers are displayed on beribboned pots of jasmine, trained onto wire loops.*

FAR LEFT: *A single, perfect bloom is one of the simplest but most beautiful ways to decorate a place setting.*

RIGHT: *Chair backs are a good vehicle for extra decoration. This delicate wreath of pompom-like mimosa adds a dash of sunny color.*

OPPOSITE, ABOVE RIGHT: *A floral ball of roses, tulips, and snowberries adds a celebratory touch to a door handle.*

OPPOSITE, BELOW LEFT: *A cluster of soft yellow spray roses sits in a silver pot to finish a gilded place setting.*

OPPOSITE, BELOW RIGHT: *To complement the floral ball shown above, posies of roses, tulips, and snowberries adorn the backs of gold chairs and double up as card holders.*

prevent everything looking jumbled. For instance, you could place little clusters of spray roses at every setting in a variety of vintage tea or coffee cups (these could also take the place of favors or double up as card holders). Empty antique perfume bottles could be put to similar use. Instead of having one large floral centerpiece per table, you could have lots of small arrangements dotted around the reception (such as the pink roses on pages 56–57) in a mixture of clear glass containers, ranging from cut-glass tumblers to bud vases. If there's an impressive mantelpiece in the room where you're having the reception, why not arrange flowers in a collection of tall, clear, glass bottles. If you're using mismatching containers, keep your flowers simple and use a single variety and color.

Galvanized metal or terracotta pots are ideal for table arrangements, and can be bought at florists or garden centers. They look particularly effective holding planted flowers, although you'll have to plant them four to six weeks before the wedding. For a winter wedding, try highly scented paper-white narcissi or, for spring, hyacinths. Alternatives include bedding plants or garden plants (such as the lily of the valley and jasmine on page 53).

glorious gold

THIS PICTURE: *Summer roses and old-fashioned pinks adorn white folding chairs at an outdoor reception.*

RIGHT: *Small posies of fragile pink dog roses have been placed in a collection of antique glassware and dotted around the room as an alternative to large set-piece arrangements.*

THIS PICTURE: *Delight your guests' senses at your reception. These fragrant, papery sweet peas, loosely tied with pale pink, candy-striped ribbon, will exude their scent throughout the meal.*

Shallow containers are very useful for displaying flower heads, snipped off right at the top of the stem. Since your guests will be able to view them at such close quarters, try something exquisitely formed such as roses, peonies, or orchids. Shallow bowls are also perfect for displays of candles and petals floating in water (see pages 128–129). Have one large container in the center of each table, or place a glass dessert bowl at each place setting containing a single bloom. Large seashells, filled with a drop of water, can be used in the same way. Goldfish bowls look spectacular filled with flower heads and petals, magnifying the blooms and exaggerating their beauty. For an informal country wedding, wicker or wire baskets could be filled with a mass of flowers, or a mixture of flowers and seasonal fruits, for table centerpieces. You could even use humble jam jars, bound with narrow gingham ribbon and filled with casual bunches of sweet peas or cornflowers.

If you want to make a big statement with your flowers, save any imposing arrangements for a

palest plums and purples

OPPOSITE, ABOVE LEFT: *Roses look particularly effective when tightly packed together to form a domed arrangement.* OPPOSITE, CENTER: *Wreaths can be used to decorate walls and doors as well as chairs. Here, variegated ivy is dotted with roses and stephanotis.* OPPOSITE, BELOW RIGHT: *Table flowers should take their cue from the overall style of the reception. Here, the reception is a formal one and the arrangements reflect this: pink roses and white stephanotis alternate to create a regular effect.* LEFT: *Make sure that chair-back wreaths—here, a composition of anemones and ivy—are securely attached with ribbon so that they don't slip when guests take their seats.*

Did you know THAT QUEEN VICTORIA'S WHITE SATIN AND HONITON LACE
WEDDING DRESS WAS TRIMMED WITH ORANGE BLOSSOM, TRADITIONALLY ASSOCIATED WITH
FERTILITY BECAUSE THE TREES FLOWER AND BEAR FRUIT AT THE SAME TIME?

OPPOSITE AND THIS PAGE: *An idyllic country garden sets the mood for a relaxed summer wedding. In keeping with the outdoors theme, garden chairs and benches have been used for seating, festooned with garlands of flowers. Garden foliage, roses, feverfew, and crab apples add to the rustic look, with arrangements spilling out of galvanized metal buckets, creating a feeling of informality and abundance.*

position where everyone can appreciate them, perhaps in an alcove or on a pedestal. One approach is to use flowers sparsely, arranging a few tall stems of striking flowers such as orchids, arum lilies, or African lilies. For a more romantic look, go for a fuller, softer arrangement such as the blowsy pink hydrangeas on page 52. A more unusual technique is to concentrate guests' eyes on the contents of the container itself. Flower stems can be anchored with smooth pebbles, glass beads, or even fruit (pears, apples, or slices of citrus fruits can work well). Experiment with filling a cylindrical container with flowers (perhaps hyacinths or grape hyacinths) so that their heads sit a ways down in the container. The glass has the effect of magnifying the flowers, drawing the eyes to them. Another clever technique is to crumple up clear cellophane (available from florists) and stuff it into a cylindrical glass vase. Push flower heads randomly into the cellophane (roses or carnations look good), then slowly fill up with water to produce a "cracked-ice" effect.

OPPOSITE AND RIGHT: *Posts and pillars are good sites for floral displays, particularly at entrances and exits. Here, the arrangement on the pillar will be the last one the bride and groom see as they leave, and will look good in photographs, too.*
LEFT AND BELOW LEFT: *A pretty wreath attached to the trunk of the honeymoon car ensures that the newlyweds will make a stylish departure.*

going away in style

Flower arrangements needn't be limited to tables alone. Chair backs can be used for further decoration and make a welcoming sight for guests. Little posies or paper cones filled with flowers can be attached with a length of ribbon (but do make sure that decorations are firmly attached so that they don't slip when guests sit down). Wreaths look good on chair backs, too, as well as suspended from door and cupboard handles, or fixed to walls, pillars, or posts. Floral balls are a pretty idea, and hung from door handles with silky ribbon immediately make an entrance look more inviting and festive. Mantelpieces, benches, and long tables all offer an opportunity to employ extravagant floral swags and garlands (see page 60).

Flowers can transform even the humblest of settings, but sadly their beauty is only temporary. Since your floral decorations will have served their purpose by the end of the wedding reception, why not encourage your guests to take them home with them? That way, while you're on your honeymoon, guests will be able to continue to enjoy their beauty for several days to come.

confetti

SHOWERING NEWLYWEDS WITH CONFETTI DATES BACK TO
ANCIENT TIMES, WHEN GRAIN WAS THROWN OVER COUPLES
TO ENSURE A FRUITFUL UNION. THIS GESTURE OF
COLLECTIVE HAPPINESS MAY HAVE LOST ITS SYMBOLISM,
BUT IT STILL SUMS UP THE JOYFUL SPIRIT OF THE DAY.

C O N F E T T I

Confetti has taken many forms over the centuries. While it seems to have started life as grain, the Romans apparently preferred to throw almonds over the happy couple. Centuries later, rice became popular, and is still sometimes used today, but tiny, colored paper shapes have taken over as the norm.

Paper confetti nowadays comes in every conceivable shape and color, but in recent years there's been a surge of interest in alternatives. Flower petals, fresh or dried, add a romantic, fairytale air to the proceedings. Roses are one of the best sources and come in a wonderful array of colors, from rich, velvety reds to satiny pinks in every hue and, of course, white. Other possibilities include sweet-smelling lavender, or delphiniums (perfect if blue is your accent color, since it's relatively rare in the flower kingdom).

Did you know THAT THE WORD "CONFETTI" IS NINETEENTH-CENTURY IN ORIGIN AND COMES FROM THE ITALIAN WORD FOR BONBON OR SWEET, A REFLECTION OF THE FACT THAT SUGAR-COATED NUTS WERE ONCE THROWN OVER NEWLYWEDS?

If you've got suitable plants in your garden (or a generous friend's), you can pick your own (first thing in the morning, when they're at their freshest). If not, flower petal confetti is available to buy. Try cherry blossom in spring, annuals such as sweet peas in summer, and hydrangeas in later summer and autumn. If you've chosen a vibrant color scheme, marigolds or gerberas might fit the bill. Birdseed is another possibility and will provide a feast for local wildlife.

O P P O S I T E : *Paper confetti comes in many shapes and colors, but check with the place you're having your reception before you throw it.*

O P P O S I T E , I N S E T : *Rosy-red rose petals, gathered from the garden and displayed in a pretty enameled bowl, beg to be scooped up by the handful.*

L E F T : *These embroidered linen sachets are ideal for confetti and could be given away as favors afterwards.*

A B O V E : *Rice or birdseed confetti is best handed around in little bags or sachets, rather than offered loose.*

THIS PICTURE: Concoct your own confetti from a mixture of flowers. This pearly-white blend includes hydrangea and rose petals.
BELOW, INSET: These embroidered silk bags, stuffed to the brim with velvety rose petals, would be a charming keepsake for the bridesmaids.

All these are biodegradable, a great advantage if your wedding is being held somewhere that bans paper confetti-throwing (something you should check). The ultimate in no-mess confetti is bubbles, which go down particularly well with children.

You may want to leave it up to your guests to bring confetti, but it adds to the fun if you provide it yourself and give a groomsman the job of handing it out after the ceremony. Present it loose in baskets or galvanized metal buckets, or package it up in little cones of decorative paper. If you're having bridesmaids, it's a nice idea to give them all a little fabric bag for confetti, which can be kept afterwards as a memento. What nicer way to start married life than under a shower of silken petals?

THIS PICTURE: *This rustic wire basket is just right for keeping cones of confetti upright. Sheets of handmade paper have been rolled into cones and filled with pink and white fabric petals. A wire-edged ribbon bow decorates the basket's handle.*

cakes

It's extraordinary just what can be conjured up out of simple flour, eggs, butter, and sugar. With patience, skill, and imagination, a humble cake can be transformed into a work of art and an impressive centerpiece for the reception.

MEMORABLE, MOUTHWATERING CAKES

The wedding cake plays a starring role at a wedding reception. It's usually given a table all of its own, carefully positioned so that guests can admire it as they make their way to their places. The cutting of the cake is a high point in the festivities and one rich in symbolism (cakes have been consumed at weddings since classical times to ensure a fruitful union).

The traditional choice is a three-layered confection, usually embellished with white royal or fondant icing. Many cakes still take this as a starting point, though tiers are now often stacked rather than balanced on columns. White has the advantage of being the perfect foil for other colors, whether bright or pale, and a backdrop against which intricate piping shows up well.

If you're going to experiment with color, do it carefully. Pastels—softest pink, blue or lilac, or cream—are the safest options, while stronger shades are usually best used as highlights (see the rose-covered cake above). Used subtly, gold, silver, or sparkling finishes add glamour (see the glittering butterfly on page 76). If you choose a cake that's dark chocolate (see right), you may want to lighten the effect with splashes of color. Reds, blues, and pinks have been used here, but these could be replaced with creams, apricots, and burnt oranges.

As for what lies beneath the icing, a rich fruit mixture is the time-honored favorite in Britain, but it could be plain pound cake or chocolate, vanilla, coffee, lemon, or carrot cake. Having one large cake makes a strong statement, and although you could

RIGHT: *Everyone loves chocolate cake, but all that luscious darkness can look unbridal. Here, a cone-shaped cake, covered in luscious chocolate frills, has been studded with vivid anemones for added contrast and color.*

have a single layer, a stacked or tiered version makes it easier to appreciate the decoration. As an alternative, an arrangement of gorgeously decorated cupcakes, one for each guest, on a series of cake stands would look stunning (see page 70). You could play around with different-colored icing and toppings of real or sugar flowers, iced hearts or initials, or candies. These could double up as favors and be presented to guests as they leave.

Icing and fondant are amazingly versatile materials and, in the hands of an expert, can be turned into virtually anything, from flowers that look like the real thing, to intricate patterns as fine as lace. Your source of inspiration may be

LEFT: *Cakes needn't be expensive, or even specially made, but if you buy something off the shelf, pay extra attention to presentation. Here, petits fours, available at specialty bakeries, have been placed on coordinating, embroidered linen doilies to act as favors, creating spots of soft color against the white tablecloth.*

THIS PAGE AND ABOVE LEFT:
A delicate posy of pink hydrangeas sits on each layer of this tiered cake. The lacy effect of the blooms harmonizes with the icing pearls defining the base of each tier.

This spectacular white chocolate cake looks irresistibly creamy and rich. The dainty embellishments add contrasting texture and movement—quivering paper butterflies on the lower tiers and a sparkling, sequined butterfly on top, nestling upon ruffled chocolate and a white-and-gold-striped ribbon.

your shared interests or something that recalls the way you met. Another approach is to echo the wedding dress itself, and mimic beading, fabric, or embroidery in icing. If traditional icing doesn't appeal, decorative alternatives include fresh fruit (perhaps frosted with sugar) and sugared almonds or other candies. Of course, decorations needn't be edible. Fresh flowers always look pretty (though make absolutely sure that they haven't been sprayed with chemicals), as do velvety rose petals, fabric flowers, braid, ribbon, and other trimmings.

Finally, don't forget the table on which the cake sits. Like a picture frame, it must show off the beautiful creation it bears. Consider using a special tablecloth, posies of flowers, or a scattering of petals or sugared almonds, and place the cake knife, tied perhaps with a beautiful ribbon, alongside two champagne flutes to anticipate the happy toasts to come.

natural abundance

ABOVE: *This very feminine square stacked cake has been covered in basketweave icing. The blowsy roses in palest pastel shades that spill over each layer enhance the cake's demure, ladylike, 1950s charm.*

table settings

GUESTS SPEND MUCH OF THE RECEPTION SEATED, SO THE
WAY TABLES ARE DECORATED CAN DO MUCH TO SET THE
MOOD AND ENCOURAGE A CONVIVIAL ATMOSPHERE. USE
CHINA, GLASSWARE, FLOWERS, AND LINENS CREATIVELY TO
MAKE YOUR TABLES A PLEASURE TO FEAST AT.

CHINA, GLASS, & SILVERWARE

A wedding reception is your opportunity to welcome and entertain your guests. It's a thank you to everyone for coming and a group celebration of a joyous occasion. Taking the time and trouble to plan attractive table settings shows how much you value your guests. The pleasure that they'll feel at seeing a beautifully laid-out table when they take their seats will do much to create a festive, celebratory atmosphere. Unlike large floral displays in a church or other location, which are designed to be seen from a distance, a table setting is viewed in close-up, so all those small details won't go unnoticed. One way to give your tables a distinctive look is to use everyday objects in unusual ways: tumblers or shot glasses for tiny posies; wine goblets or glass dessert bowls for floating single blooms in; floral teacups or glass cake stands for displaying boxed favors.

Color is a good place to start when planning your table settings. Your scheme should complement the bridal flowers and dress to give the day a coordinated look. An all-white scheme is easy to put together and will work best if there are plenty of different textures—embossed china, heavy damask table linen, diaphanous ribbon napkin rings, fresh roses, and so on. For an even less colorful, almost ethereal look, you could focus on transparency, with glass or plexiglass taking a

BELOW: These garden tables have been covered with dainty, old-fashioned, hand-embroidered tablecloths. The favors (in the background) have been tied with a variety of colorful ribbons, to pick up the colors used in the embroidery.

OPPOSITE, ABOVE, AND THIS PAGE: *This romantic table setting features antique floral plates combined with plain white china. The pattern on the plates inspired a wedding color scheme of gold, blue, and pink, which is repeated in the flowers, liqueur glasses, and ribbon-tied roses that lie upon each plate.*

THIS PAGE: *Pistachio green, palest pink, and white is the scheme that unites this table setting. The scalloped plates are complemented by the napkins, which have been tied with floral braid. The white tablecloth has been overlaid with embroidered muslin bearing the same motif.*

OPPOSITE, ABOVE: *A wire garland of green glass hearts has been laid across each plate at this setting—a romantic touch that enhances the green detail on the china.*

starring role (see pages 90–91). Even with a white scheme, however, introducing interest in the form of touches of color such as green, silver, or gold is very effective (see pages 84 and 87). Pastel colors work well together and, of course, with white. Using rich, dark colors is a bold choice and can look magnificent (see page 88), but it needs to be done with restraint.

Whatever your featured colors, the backdrop to a table setting is always the table itself, or rather what goes on top of it—the table linen. Tablecloths and napkins can be cotton, linen, or a man-made mixture, and come in a variety of weaves or finishes, the classic choice being damask. Table linen can be rented in a rainbow of colors as well as whites, ivories, and creams. A neutral backdrop is the easiest to work with, but colored napkins can look very pretty, particularly if one or two pastel shades are contrasted with a white cloth. Napkins themselves are astonishingly versatile and can be dressed up in all sorts of ways to turn them into decorative features in their own right (see pages 92–99). For extra interest on the table, cloths can be

feminine florals....

RIGHT: *This plexiglass-handled flatware is a departure from the norm and would look good with any white table setting.*
FAR RIGHT: *A color scheme may be prompted by the finest detail. Here, it's the blue border of this Italian china.*

THIS PAGE: *An engraved glass pear makes an exquisite focal point. The pear is decorated with an organza ribbon scattered with gold stars, which accentuates the gilt border on the plates.*
OPPOSITE, ABOVE LEFT: *A silver cake knife is dressed up with a large, floppy bow.*

BELOW: *If you have access to just a few pieces of beautiful family silverware, such as this embossed knife and fork, why not use them for the place settings on the top table?*

layered, with the top ones being laid diagonally to create a diamond pattern. Alternatively, runners can be placed over tablecloths to add texture, pattern, and color. Sheer fabrics, patterned or embroidered (see page 82), are pretty, or try experimenting with organza or shantung for a glamorous effect.

Most receptions involve a meal, and the china it is served on should show off the food as well as create a decorative effect. Much of the china available is plain white or has a fine gold or silver rim, styles that are effective foils for any color scheme. Hunting down decorative tableware may be more difficult, although good catering companies and party planners often have access to less run-of-the-mill designs. If your wedding is a small one, you may be able to take advantage of your own or your family's china collections. Mixing and matching china in what is

Did you know THAT TRADITIONALLY THE MOST POPULAR TIME OF THE YEAR TO MARRY WAS BETWEEN SEPTEMBER AND CHRISTMAS, WHEN FOOD WAS AT ITS MOST PLENTIFUL?

OPPOSITE: *A gleaming silver pot is an elegant and gracious way to serve coffee. Petits fours, arranged on an antique silver cake stand, are a deliciously pretty accompaniment.*

THIS PICTURE AND INSET: *Patterned glasses add interest to the table. For this sophisticated table setting, silver-edged china determines the theme. Sheer metallic ribbon and modern flatware finish the look.*

RIGHT: *Using deep, rich colors against a white backdrop makes a strong statement that does not become overpowering. Pinky-red flowers, china, glassware, and candles give this table setting a grand, dramatic character that is still pretty and feminine.*

OPPOSITE, LEFT: *Distinctive glassware makes a subtle but unmistakable decorative contribution to the table.*

OPPOSITE, RIGHT: *A pink-rimmed, antique glass dish holds a tempting array of sugared almonds, bringing height and pretty pastel tones to the table.*

called a harlequin setting can look very charming and would suit an informal style of reception. Another effective way of using china is to combine plain white with a patterned charger (a large underplate on which the rest of the setting is placed). If the only china available to you is plain and you want a more decorative effect, make full use of napkins and napkin rings, ribbons, or fresh flowers, placed on top of the plates. Don't limit yourself to plates and bowls when you're choosing tableware. You can use candlesticks; decorative dishes, bowls, and cake stands; pretty cups for coffee; even elaborate condiment sets.

Glassware adds welcome height to a table setting and often color and pattern, too. Glass can be etched, embossed, or engraved for subtle or ornate effects, and styles with tinted stems or bowls can be useful for reinforcing color schemes. Wineglass or champagne flute stems are good places for adding decoration—ribbon, beads, or flowers—and securing name

Did you know THAT FOR TOASTS, THE GLASS SHOULD BE RAISED IN THE RIGHT HAND AND HELD OUT STRAIGHT FROM THE SHOULDER? THIS MEDIEVAL PRACTICE DEMONSTRATED THAT THE TOASTER WAS NOT CONCEALING WEAPONS IN HIS CLOTHING, PROVING THAT HE CAME IN FRIENDSHIP.

tags. They can even be used for placing favors in (see pages 112 and 122). You may want to use glass vases for your table flowers; if you do, make sure they're not so tall or large that they'll prevent eye contact between guests across the table.

Flatware is often given little thought, but the style you choose needs to complement the rest of the setting, particularly if you're going for a minimalist look, which will demand something equally sleek and simple. Most rental companies provide flatware of traditional design, which complements most table settings with an element of formality. If you have access to family silver but not in sufficient quantity to set at every place, reserve it for the head table or the bride and groom's places to mark them out as special. The cake knife plays an important symbolic role at the reception (using it is supposed to be the newlyweds' first joint act together), so you might want to dress it up with a bow (see page 85).

Attractive presentation of your reception tables will greatly enhance everyone's enjoyment of the day, enabling your guests to feast their eyes while they fill their stomachs. Even if the elements at your disposal are plain and simple, clever embellishment with napkins, flowers, and favors will take them out of the ordinary and turn them into something memorable.

OPPOSITE AND THIS PAGE, BELOW LEFT AND CENTER: *A collection of pressed-glass plates, cups, and saucers, accompanied by flatware with ornate, colored-glass handles, and finely decorated crystal dishes, creates the most delicate and ethereal of table settings.* THIS PAGE, BOTTOM RIGHT: *A gossamer-fine, wire garland of tiny glass hearts casts delicate shadows on a silver-rimmed plate.*

crystal clear

ABOVE: *A napkin has been made into a
fan (fold in half, then half again, then nip
in one corner with ribbon) and decorated
with tiny crab apples, for which any small
fruits (kumquats or red currants, perhaps)
or flowers could be substituted.*

NAPKINS

Although napkins serve a straightforwardly practical purpose (particularly on a
day when everyone is dressed in their finery), they can be turned into a highly
decorative part of the table setting.

In the seventeenth century, it became the practice to use large white
napkins on formal occasions such as weddings. A starched white or cream
napkin in damask or plain-weave linen, as generously proportioned as
possible, remains the classic choice. Linen double damask is considered the
finest quality since it is self-patterned on both sides of the fabric. Although
white is the obvious wedding color for table linen, providing an ideal backdrop
for the table setting, using colored napkins is a way of personalizing the
tablescape. Pastels, such as candy pink, baby blue, or pistachio green, look
romantic and summery and could work well if they pick up on an accent color
used for the wedding dress or flowers. For an autumnal wedding, you might

OPPOSITE, ABOVE RIGHT: *Lengths of ready-made ruffled white ribbon have been joined to make these feminine napkin rings.*

THIS PAGE: *Scour fabric and craft stores for interesting braids, buttons, ribbons, and other notions, which can be transformed into unique decorative napkin rings.*

golden wedding

ABOVE: *Cream napkins, embellished with slender gilt hoops, sit on a burnished plate.* ABOVE RIGHT: *A special napkin ring would make a lovely present for a bridesmaid or mother on the big day. This beautiful, delicate napkin ring looks like a piece of precious jewelry.*

want all the table linen to reflect the rich, warm colors of the season. In summer, the intensity of the light means that it's easier to get away with vibrant brights. Your napkins don't have to match your tablecloth and you might want to use them to introduce an element of pattern or contrasting color. Whatever colors or patterns you choose, think about how they will work with the food you are serving. One should complement the other.

The classic way to present napkins is to fold them into a rectangle and to rest them on plates so that they just overlap the top and bottom. Whether the napkins lie in the middle of the place setting or to one side is up to you. There are more elaborate approaches to napkin folding. In the seventeenth century there was a fashion for creating extraordinary shapes—animals, birds, butterflies—and professional napkin folders would work their magic in wealthy households in preparation for grand banquets. While such things are beyond most of us, it's easy to fold napkins into pockets (see page 99) so that place

BELOW: *An extravagant beaded tassel brings instant glamour.*
RIGHT: *A pewter bowl holds napkins, each rolled up inside silver fretwork rings with place cards attached.*
BELOW RIGHT: *Classic white china with a silver border is coordinated with napkins tied with shimmering silver ribbon.*

THIS PAGE: *Elegant silk tassels adorned with the softest mink pompoms (designed, in fact, as keyrings) make the ultimate in luxurious—and sensual—napkin rings.*

Did you know THAT IN THE MIDDLE AGES THE SIZE OF A GUEST'S NAPKIN INDICATED THEIR WEALTH AND SOCIAL STATUS? THE RICHEST COULD AFFORD LARGE, LUXURIOUS NAPKINS, WHICH WERE OFTEN EMBROIDERED.

cards, flowers, breadsticks, or other decorations can be popped in. Another easy arrangement is to fold napkins into triangles and then roll them up, which also creates a pocket. Napkins can be cinched in the middle (see page 99), or turned into little fans (see page 92), though the easiest way to display them is simply to roll them up and secure them with a ring. If you want your napkins elaborately folded by your caterers, they will have to be well starched to hold their shape.

Decorating napkins opens up a world of possibilities, from the elaborate to the simple. Lots of the best effects can be achieved with everyday materials and minimal effort. Napkins that have been folded into rectangles and placed on plates can be embellished with single flowers to romantic effect. Fresh herbs such as lavender or rosemary can be used, or perhaps homemade cookies, cut into hearts. Fruits also look effective, as do daisy chains, rose petals, and sugared almonds.

One of the easiest and prettiest ways to secure your napkins is to roll them up and tie decorative ribbon around them. Wide ribbon can be turned into napkin rings, as can lace, braid, cord, or other

ABOVE LEFT: *Roses and weddings go hand in hand. This white porcelain rose and the napkin it encircles create a look of pure, timeless elegance.* LEFT: *Upholstery braid has been used here as a napkin ring. The pretty flower motif picks up a theme of pistachio green, pink, and white, which is repeated throughout the table setting.*

delicate details

trims (see page 93). Wire-edged ribbon is particularly good as it holds its shape so well. Look for interesting materials in fabric and craft stores. Beads could be threaded onto wire, ribbon, or yarn to make napkin rings. Consider using shells, pearly buttons, and tassels in the same way. Thrift stores can also yield surprising finds, such as old crystal chandeliers, whose droplets can be threaded and tied around napkins, or vintage costume jewelry. Homemade cookies can be threaded onto ribbon (pierce holes in them before baking). Your napkins could also be encircled by stems of ivy or blades of long, strong grass, such as bear grass (available from your florist), or chives.

Even with something as commonplace and utilitarian as napkins, there's lots of fun to be had by turning them into a decorative feature on the table. Your guests will then have the pleasurable job of unfolding them in preparation for the feasting that's to follow.

ABOVE: *A neat row of embroidered napkins awaits the cutting of the cake, with pastry forks slipped beneath napkin rings of pink ribbon.* ABOVE RIGHT: *Three variations on a white-on-white theme: a shell threaded onto ribbon; a button on ribbon; and a satin-bound pipe cleaner clasping a single perfect pearl.*

THIS PAGE: *Folding napkins can create pretty effects. The left-hand napkin was folded in half, then into three, and tied with ribbon. The middle one has been folded diagonally and cinched with a fabric rose. On the right, the napkin has been made into a pouch, with a place card slipped in.*

Claudia

PLACE CARDS & TABLE NUMBERS

Drawing up a seating plan for the reception can be one of the most taxing and time-consuming parts of pre-wedding planning. Trying to choreograph things so that old friends will have a chance to catch up, new friendships will be forged, and relatives won't feel left out can tie everyone in knots. However, it's the best way to avoid an unseemly scramble for places and disappointed guests. Once the hard work is out of the way, reward yourself by having fun displaying your place cards and table numbers. Even though they're a small detail, they're an important one, helping to set the tone for the feast to come and ensure that everyone knows where they're going.

If you've got attractive handwriting, you could pen the cards yourself. It's worth getting hold of a proper fountain pen for the purpose, or buying a calligraphy kit. Black ink will read most clearly, but you could choose sepia for a soft, romantic look, or brightly colored inks, perhaps using one color for male guests and another for female. Stationers and art stores sell metallic pens, though these inks are sometimes less visible from a distance.

The classic hands for formal stationery are italic, the elegant script developed in the Vatican at the end of the fifteenth century; and copperplate, a

Did you know THAT THE ORIGIN OF THE TERM "HONEYMOON" IS THE OLD PRACTICE OF NEWLYWEDS DRINKING MEAD—SYMBOLIC OF LIFE AND FERTILITY, AND MADE FROM FERMENTED HONEY—FOR A MONTH AFTER THEIR WEDDING?

OPPOSITE: *This ivy wreath is decked with paper leaves, held in place with gilt butterflies, on which names and table numbers are written in gold.*

ABOVE RIGHT: *A place card, decorated with a little white rose (like those available from fabric and craft stores), is tied to the lid of a soup cup.*

BELOW LEFT: *The slender stem of a wineglass is an obvious place to tie a place card. Secure them with wire, ribbon, or braid.*

BELOW RIGHT: *You may be lucky enough to have decorative objects with which to dress your tables. Here, an exquisite porcelain pagoda holds a votive candle and acts as a table marker.*

fine hand based on that used in copperplate engravings from the seventeenth century onwards. A computer is a quicker option, and has the advantage of being easier to correct mistakes on. Most programs seem to have a huge array of fonts, from the classic to the wacky. The other option is to have the place cards printed along with the wedding invitations, or to commission a professional calligrapher. Whichever method you choose, make sure the writing is easy to decipher, even from some distance. If your wedding is small and intimate, you may be able to get away with using first names alone for the place cards, but for a larger gathering, write the guests' names in full. Don't forget to put someone in charge of a master copy of the seating plan, just in case any cards get dropped or otherwise mislaid.

The usual material for place cards is white or cream card stock, but you could alternatively use a pastel color, particularly if it ties in with detail on the wedding dress or the bouquets. Another possibility is heavy or textured paper.

teatime treats

THIS PAGE: *For this immaculate white-on-white setting, napkins have been tied in the middle with gold ribbon and draped over the plates. The place cards sit above and just to the left of each plate, held in silver card holders.*

You could even write the names (preferably in white or a metallic ink) on thick, glossy leaves, such as laurel. To give place cards an individual touch, experiment with patterned craft scissors or pinking shears to produce a decorative edge.

You'll need not only to put a card at each place setting but also to display a seating plan. The simplest way to do this is to print one out on a piece of paper, grouping guests' names under each lettered or numbered table. However, it adds to the fun to approach it a bit more creatively. The formal custom is to have small envelopes bearing the name of each guest, with the table number written on a card inside. For a more relaxed feel, you could have folded or tented cards with both the name and table number on them. Set out the cards on a large table so that more than one person at a time can collect them, somewhere near the entrance to the reception. It looks very elegant to lay the cards out in neat rows, perhaps along lengths of wide ribbon that have been pinned to the tablecloth. You could ask your florist to make you a floral "cushion" for them to rest on by inserting flowers, their stems

ABOVE LEFT: *This simple idea gains its impact by being executed on a grand scale. Champagne flutes, in ordered rows, each hold a single flower, to whose stem an escort card has been tied.*
ABOVE RIGHT: *This pearl-beaded number "2" was shaped from wire and nestles in a bed of sugared almonds to make a delectable centerpiece.*

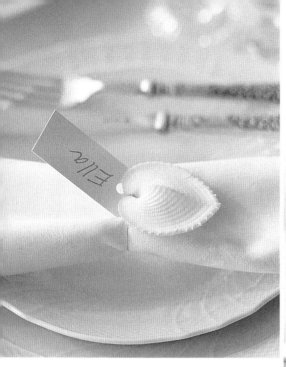

OPPOSITE: *White baby pumpkins, available in late summer, are an unusual choice of card holder but have great rustic charm.*

ABOVE: *White and silver combine to make a subtle color scheme. The napkins are cinched in with wire, with a heart-shaped shell ornament and name tag attached.*

ABOVE CENTER: *You may want to invest in special place-card holders for the top table as mementos of the day. This delightful porcelain bunny would undoubtedly become a treasured keepsake.*

ABOVE RIGHT: *Table-top easels can be bought from art stores and are the right size for holding table numbers. Here, the numbers have been written in gold to echo the gold border on the china.*

simple pleasures

snipped very short, into a block of florist's foam. You could turn place cards into little flags, attach them to toothpicks and stick them into individual chocolates or cupcakes, or attach them to small boxes of candies, wrapped with ribbon. In this way, place cards can double up as favors for guests to take home with them. There's no reason why you shouldn't display place cards on a wall, as the elegant wreath on page 100 shows.

Exercise your inventiveness at place settings, too. Place cards can be attached to little boxes of favors, or to the stems of wineglasses. They could sit in pretty coffee cups; be tucked into napkins, or between the layers of pine cones (perhaps sprayed gold or silver); be tied to sprigs of lavender or the stems of roses; or attached to pieces of flatware with decorative ribbon. Place-card holders can be purchased at stores or on websites that sell bridal products, and can double up as favors to be taken home by the guests.

Did you know THAT UNTIL THE LATE NINETEENTH CENTURY WEDDINGS WERE HELD IN THE MORNING, SO THE MEAL SERVED AT A WEDDING IS STILL KNOWN AS THE WEDDING BREAKFAST?

Table numbers must be a good size and clearly displayed, and they could form part of a larger centerpiece. Whether you use letters of the alphabet or numbers is up to you, but be sure that you stick to one system—numbers on the seating plan and letters on the tables could cause a traffic jam. For a country wedding, you could draw numbers in chalk on little slates, or make jaunty paper flags, glued to kabob skewers, and stick them into jam jars filled with sand and shells. For a more sophisticated approach, numbers could be made by threading beads onto wire. A skilled baker could fashion numbers out of bread or pretzel dough, while an accomplished cake maker or confectioner could even create them out of pulled sugar.

Although place cards and table numbers are some of the finer points of reception detail, they're fun to exercise your inventiveness on and they help, in however small a way, to make the day a memorable one.

ABOVE AND BELOW LEFT: *Flowers in miniature pots make charming place-card holders, adding height, color, and, in some cases, scent to the table. Try small bulbs, such as grape hyacinths or dwarf narcissi, or potted plants, such as lily of the valley, cyclamen, or African violets.*

OPPOSITE AND LEFT: *This spectacular green-on-green centerpiece uses glass balls (try Christmas decorations), on which the table number has been written in thick silver pen, and bunches of grapes on the vine, all piled onto a crystal dish.*

favors

PRESENTING GUESTS WITH A PARTING GIFT AS A MEMENTO OF THE DAY IS AN AGE-OLD TRADITION. WHETHER IT'S A BAG OF HOMEMADE COOKIES OR SOMETHING MORE PERMANENT, A THOUGHTFUL PRESENT WILL BE SURE TO BRING A SMILE TO EVERYONE'S FACE.

ABOVE: *Silk flowers and floral ribbon make these favor boxes a gift in themselves.*
ABOVE CENTER: *A cheerful assortment of ribbons adds to the festive effect of favors piled on a dish.*
ABOVE RIGHT: *Placing this beribboned favor in a glass that echoes the blue of the ribbon heightens its visual impact.*

MEMENTOS & KEEPSAKES

Favors—little gifts for guests to take home with them—have enjoyed a huge rise in popularity in recent years. However, there's nothing new about the concept, which has its roots in classical civilization. In ancient Rome, guests broke bread over the heads of the bride and groom before picking up pieces and eating them, a practice which, centuries later, evolved into the tradition of having a wedding cake. Taking home a slice of this cake and taking home a favor have the same symbolic meaning—they are a token shared between the newlyweds and their family and friends, reflecting the guests' role in witnessing and supporting the marriage. In time, favors evolved into a gift of five sugared almonds (also known as Jordan almonds, or *bomboniere*) to represent health, wealth, long life, happiness, and fertility. Almonds have had a long association with weddings due to their link with fruitfulness and abundance. There is also the idea that a bitter almond with a sweet coating reflects the wedding vow "for better or for worse." Nowadays, favors can be any small gift, distributed as a thank you to guests for their attendance and to remind them of the wedding.

THIS PAGE: *Tiny, hand-painted enameled boxes, tied with pastel ribbons, make exquisite, extravagant keepsakes that can be personalized with the date of the wedding or initials of the bride and groom.*

Did you know THAT THE IDEA OF GIVING GIFTS TO GUESTS GOES BACK HUNDREDS OF YEARS? AT HIGH-SOCIETY WEDDINGS IN THE NINETEENTH CENTURY, GUESTS WERE GIVEN SUCH THINGS AS SCARVES, GLOVES, AND GARTERS.

All this symbolism aside, wedding favors are great fun to plan, and are a detail that will charm and surprise your guests. They needn't be fancy or expensive; merely thoughtfully chosen. You could give out little bundles of slender candles, bound with wide ribbon; tiny lanterns (finished with a ribbon bow); or boxes of scented candles. Little sachets of potpourri or dried lavender are another sweet-smelling idea. For a gift which will delight guests months after the wedding, wrap up packets of seeds (easy-to-grow annuals, such as sweet peas or larkspur, for instance) or place bulbs in cardboard boxes (including planting instructions). Embroidered handkerchiefs, scented soaps, or miniature books are other good possibilities. If your wedding has a strong seasonal slant, select the favors accordingly: perhaps painted or dyed eggs in spring; paper fans for summer; apple- or pear-shaped candles in autumn; and bundles of mulled wine spices, snow globes, or Christmas tree balls in winter. Small terracotta or galvanized metal pots, with bulbs or houseplants planted in them, make charming favors and, like many of the other ideas here, can double up as place markers.

OPPOSITE AND THIS PAGE: *Enveloping a favor in a lacy or embroidered handkerchief, which can be personalized with the bride and groom's initials, means that the lovely wrapping becomes part of the gift. Add a ribbon bow or a dainty fabric rose as a finishing touch.*

pretty parcels

Once you've chosen your favors, you can decide how you'd like to package them. Little envelopes are useful for loose items such as seeds. Seal them with sealing wax for a traditional look, or tie with pretty ribbon, then lay them in neat rows for guests to collect. Small cardboard boxes are easy to decorate and look very enticing when placed at place settings, piled onto serving dishes, or laid out neatly on trays or tables. Ribbons are a simple, inexpensive, and versatile form of decoration for favor boxes. Either choose one color of ribbon that links up with the rest of your color scheme, or use one color for male guests' favors and another for female, or go for a cheerful assortment of designs (see page 112). Boxes can be adorned with all sorts of trims and braids. Real, paper, or fabric flowers look lavishly romantic, while sparkling beads, feathers, and sequins provide a glamorous finish. You could also experiment with many different ways of wrapping your boxes, using layers of paper or tissue, bows, and ribbon (see page 120).

How and when you give out your favors is a matter of personal taste. If you want favors to be a parting gift, then station some groomsmen or staff at the exits to the reception with trays of goodies, or arrange them on a large table. You could display your favors formally, laid out in neat rows, perhaps along

ABOVE: *Your favors should continue the wedding color scheme. Here, pink and green are key colors, picked up by the fresh roses and ribbon embellishing the favors. The sparkling beads are a final, lavish touch.*
ABOVE RIGHT: *Attendants clutch their favors, tied with pastel ribbons, undoubtedly eager to see what's inside.*
OPPOSITE: *Arranged en masse, these favor boxes, topped with a fabric rose and pink ribbon, look beguilingly pretty.*

THIS PICTURE: *This gilded table setting demands equally glamorous favors. Gold boxes finished with an oversized white satin bow look just the part.*

RIGHT: *A diaphanous silk and organza flower sitting in a translucent onyx dish acts as both favor and table decoration.*

THIS PICTURE: *Another extravagant variation on the golden theme: this time a flourish of wire-edged polka-dot ribbon tops the favor box, and is finished with a fabric flower.*

LEFT: *White baby pumpkins, sporting tiny organza bows and piled into a glass serving dish, make an unusual centerpiece and whimsical favors.*
BELOW: *Different widths and shades of metallic ribbon make this favor box look sleek, smart, and modern.*

runners of wide ribbon, pinned to a tablecloth, or on top of a scattering of rose petals. For a more informal look, they could be piled into large, shallow bowls or baskets, or stacked on cake stands, with flowers tucked in between the favors for extra decoration. With the addition of place cards, favors also work well as place markers, and add a decorative touch to the table when placed on top of each plate. This is a particularly good approach if you're providing something with which guests can amuse themselves during the meal, such as bottles of bubbles. You could also include a specially created party game for everyone to try over coffee, such as coming up with anagrams of the bride and groom's names. To emphasize the idea of favors as a thank you, you could ask your bridesmaids to circulate during the reception bearing baskets of treats, handing them out table by table.

A wedding is a hugely enjoyable occasion for guests and also one at which they express their fondness for the bride and groom through the giving of gifts. Favors are a way of making this reciprocal. Whether yours are large or small, simple or extravagant, they'll delight and surprise all who receive them.

Did you know
THAT THE TRADITIONAL CHOICE FOR FAVORS IS SUGARED ALMONDS, PARTICULARLY IN ITALY, WHERE THEY'RE CALLED BOMBONIERE? FIVE ALMONDS ARE GIVEN TO EACH GUEST, REPRESENTING HEALTH, WEALTH, FERTILITY, HAPPINESS, AND LONG LIFE.

THIS PAGE: *Still life in white: a cake box tied with organza ribbon and a fabric flower is presented to guests as a romantic reminder of the day.*

EDIBLE FAVORS

Sugared or Jordan almonds are the traditional way to tempt wedding guests. Almonds have been a delicacy since ancient times—the Greeks and Romans turned them into sweetmeats by coating them in honey. They're a good choice because they last well and look decorative, coming in a rainbow of colors from pastels to metallics. They're very attractive scattered on tables like confetti or piled into little shallow dishes.

However, anything sweet can be turned into favors, from kitsch but cute conversation hearts to sophisticated chocolates (if you choose the latter, keep them cool until the last minute so that there's no risk of melting). Cookies are appealing, particularly if they are handmade or personalized with guests' initials in pale pink or blue icing. Wedding-cake-shaped cookies, iced to mimic the real thing, will prompt admiring comments from their recipients. Many professional cake makers now make miniature wedding cakes as favors—or dessert—which look spectacular on each plate. Alternatively, you could package up slices of the real wedding cake in boxes and hand them to guests as they leave (see page 121).

FAR LEFT:
Mouthwatering pink truffles are presented in a china soup bowl, packaged in cellophane, and tied with striped gold and white ribbon.
LEFT: *Bags of candies, tied with satin ribbon and placed in china cups to mark the end of the meal, make a pretty composition of pink and white.*
ABOVE: *What could be more symbolic of marriage than two gold-wrapped chocolate hearts in a champagne glass?*

THIS PAGE: *A dish of delights: candy is a good-value choice for favors if you're on a tight budget, and can easily be dressed up with ribbons, bags, and boxes to create tempting little treats.*

THIS PAGE: *Handmade chocolates packaged in an illustrated box have an old-fashioned charm that is emphasized by placing them on a lace doily.*

Did you know THAT IN VICTORIAN TIMES, IT WAS BELIEVED THAT IF AN UNMARRIED FEMALE GUEST SLEPT WITH WEDDING CAKE BENEATH HER PILLOW, SHE WOULD DREAM OF HER FUTURE HUSBAND?

Traditional treats such as old-fashioned candies or marzipan shapes are always well received, or you could go all-out for fun with multicolored jelly beans or huge, transparent lollipops, stuck in among a bowl of flowers and placed in the middle of each table. Candy and cookies are easy to package prettily. Arrange them in little tissue-paper-lined boxes, or place them in the middle of circles of cellophane, net, or organza, and gather up the edges, tying with ribbon and finishing with a real or fabric flower. Wedding companies sell fabric bags and little aluminium tins, ideal for a handful of mints or Hershey's Kisses. Although favors are usually something guests take home with them, you might want to offer edible goodies with coffee and have the pleasure of seeing your guests indulging their sweet tooth.

ABOVE LEFT: *Assorted candies, wrapped in jewel-toned twists of tissue paper, fill pretty antique coffee cups to the brim.*
ABOVE: *Carefully packaged in pink paper and topped with tiny paper roses, this Italian marzipan cake looks almost too good to eat.*

candles

IT'S IMPOSSIBLE NOT TO BE MESMERIZED AND FASCINATED
BY DANCING FLAMES. CANDLES ARE AN INDISPENSABLE
AND VERSATILE TOOL IN THE DECORATOR'S REPERTOIRE,
LOOKING GOOD WHATEVER THE STYLE OF WEDDING AND
BATHING EVERYTHING IN A WARM, WELCOMING GLOW.

CANDLES

What are weddings about if they are not about romance, and what is more romantic than flickering candlelight? Candles bring with them echoes of previous ages, of magic and otherworldliness, as well as religious symbolism and associations with innocence, purity, hope, and truth. On a purely aesthetic level, candlelight is softer and more yellow than daylight and is highly flattering, bathing its surroundings in a reassuring, welcoming glow. For all these reasons and more, candles are a beautiful addition to any wedding reception.

If you want to use candles, you must consider safety, particularly as there will be veils and children about, so discuss your plans with staff at the reception site or tent company. Moreover, if you're using candles in quantity, you'll need a way to light them all quickly (professionals often use butane torches). Another consideration is how long you want the candles to burn for. Beeswax candles burn more slowly than paraffin-based ones, and are more expensive as a result. However, you should get three or four hours of illumination even from votives.

ABOVE LEFT: Pink floating candles and petals and red roses make a colorful centerpiece.
ABOVE: Frosted-glass votives holding scented candles sit on a paper-doily-covered tray.
BELOW: A crystal cup, decorated with two lovebirds, holds a candle for the bride and groom.

THIS PAGE: *Votive candles in dainty glass holders are clustered on a circular mirror that reflects and intensifies their twinkling light.*
INSET: *Pure white candles and eucharis lily florets float serenely in a porcelain bowl.*

THIS PAGE: *A mantelpiece holds a collection of different candles and vintage holders, some decorated with glass beads, along with a lacy puff of white hydrangea for a sparkling, magical display.*

Did you know THAT CHIMNEY SWEEPS ARE TRADITIONALLY
ASSOCIATED WITH THE HEARTH AND HOME AND THAT IT'S CONSIDERED LUCKY
FOR THE BRIDE TO BE KISSED BY ONE ON HER WAY TO THE CEREMONY?

BELOW: *A large, scented candle sits on a
crystal candlestick decorated with an elaborate
wreath of paper flowers and wired beads.*
RIGHT: *Paper flowers and a large bow have
been added to an antique silver candelabrum and
candlesticks for this romantic table setting.*

Candles seem to be available almost anywhere in myriad
colors, shapes, and sizes. Whatever your wedding theme or style,
you'll find candles to match, in shapes from fruits and flowers to
cubes, pillars, and spheres. Scented candles are popular but
need to be used sensitively at a reception. Don't burn anything
that will compete with the food you're serving, such as
powerfully scented aromatherapy candles; you're safer with floral
perfumes such as rose, jasmine, or lily. Votive candles are the
most economical option and can easily be bought in bulk.
They're simple and unpretentious but, particularly when used on
a grand scale, look enchanting. Pillar candles are a classic
choice and lend themselves to elegant displays (such as the
fireplace on page 22). Floating candles are ideal for table
centerpieces and can often be found in pretty shapes such as

a glorious glow

stars, shells, or flowers. You'll need tall, slender candles if you're using candlesticks or candelabra, and you may also come across very fine tapers which, like votives, look best when arranged en masse.

Decorative candle holders and containers serve the practical purpose of enclosing the flame. Traditional candlesticks and candelabra, whether crystal, china, silver, or wrought iron, can be embellished with garlands of flowers or ivy, or lengths of beaded wire. Plain- or frosted-glass votives will enhance any setting. Homey versions can be made from jam jars, wrapped around with sheer fabric or thin paper to diffuse the light, or trimmed with ivy. Moroccan-style gilded tealights add glamour and cast pools of colored light. Lanterns come in many guises and are a good choice for outdoors, shielding the flames from wind. They look magical at night, edging a path or dotted along a wall.

If you want candles on your tables, tiny flickering votives or tealights are an obvious choice. For large-scale impact, group votives together on a tray or mirror (see pages 128–129). For table centerpieces, displays of floating

ABOVE: *White rice—which could be replaced with coffee beans, white pebbles, or glass nuggets—holds chunky cream candles in place inside straight-sided glass bowls. For an outdoor reception, citronella candles and garden flares will help keep insects at bay.*

LEFT AND OPPOSITE: *Votives burn brightly in glass lanterns suspended at different heights with colored ribbons.*
RIGHT: *Tiny votives trimmed with circles of ivy illuminate a path for guests.*

THIS PAGE: *These sleek modern candle holders can be filled with anything decorative—glass beads or flowers, perhaps. The addition of a place card has turned them into place markers.*

candles are safe and beautiful to look at and can be created in any sort of broad, shallow dish or bowl. Goldfish bowls look good, too, filled with flower heads, petals, and floating candles. Candlesticks and candelabra work well on tables (see page 131), keeping flames safely raised and allowing guests to talk around them, but they're also tailor-made for displays on mantelpieces or side tables. Another approach to decorating a mantelpiece is to collect a number of candles and holders and arrange them as a glowing, atmospheric still life.

Candles look good indoors or out, whether a wedding is formal or informal, traditional or modern. Like flowers, candles instantly create a celebratory and romantic atmosphere. Moreover, their beauty comes at a reasonable price, so—even if you buy no more than a few bags of votives—you'll be guaranteed your own enchanted evening.

Did you know THAT PURE BEESWAX CANDLES BURN CLEANER AND BRIGHTER THAN STANDARD CANDLES, DON'T DRIP OR SMOKE, AND LAST LONGER? AS WELL AS HAVING A SWEET AROMA, THEY PRODUCE NEGATIVE IONS AND THEREFORE HELP TO CLEAN THE AIR.

ABOVE: *For a winter wedding reception, paper leaves, handwritten with guests' names and table numbers, have been attached with wire to an ivy wreath that encircles a large, three-wick candle.*
RIGHT: *A pretty bow gives a fretwork lantern a festive air.*
FAR RIGHT: *White wire lanterns, hung with sparkling glass beads, hang from trees and shrubs in a summer garden.*

SOURCES

BRIDAL FASHION & ACCESSORIES

AMSALE
625 Madison Avenue
New York, NY 10022
212-583-1700
Call 800-765-0170 or visit
www.amsale.com for
a retailer near you.
Grand couture gowns and bridesmaid attire.

BADGLEY MISCHKA
525 Seventh Avenue,
11th Floor
New York, NY 10018
Call 212-921-1585
for a retailer near you.
Glamorous, heavily-beaded, high-fashion gowns.

CAROLINA AMATO
Call 212-768-9095 or visit
www.carolinaamato.com
for a retailer near you.
Luxurious gloves, veils, wraps, and handbags.

ELIZABETH FILLMORE
Call 212-647-0863 for
a retailer near you.
Sexy, glamorous, high-fashion gowns.

FENAROLI FOR REGALIA
501 Seventh Avenue
Suite 301
New York, NY 10018
212-764-5924
Visit www.fenaroli.com for
details of their other two
stores or a retailer near you.
Shoes, headpieces, veils, and accessories.

JENNIFER LEIGH
1200 Harris Avenue, 3rd Floor
Bellingham, WA 98225
Call 360-714-0992 or visit
www.jenniferleighbridal.com
for a retailer near you.
Veils and headpieces.

JOAN CALABRESE
1101 Sussex Boulevard,
Lower Level, Broomall, PA 19008
Call 610-604-0900 or visit
www.joancalabrese.net
for a retailer near you.
Flower girl dresses.

KLEINFELD
8202 Fifth Avenue
Brooklyn, NY 11209
718-765-8500
www.kleinfeldbridal.com
Full-service bridal salon with huge selection, hard-to-find designers, and experienced staff.

MANOLO BLAHNIK
31 West 54th Street
New York, NY 10019
Call 212-582-3007 for
a retailer near you.

MONIQUE LHUILLIER
9609 South Santa Monica
Boulevard
Beverly Hills, CA 90210
310-550-3388
Call 310-559-4599 or visit
www.moniquelhuillier.com
for a retailer near you.
Upscale, sexy, fashion-forward gowns.

REEM ACRA SALON
14 East 60th Street
New York, NY 10022
212-308-8760

Call 212-414-0980 or visit
www.reemacra.com for
a retailer near you.
Grand, lavishly-embroidered gowns.

SERAFINA BRIDAL
25 West 36th Street, 4th Floor
New York, NY 10018
212-253-2754
www.serafina.net
Excellent selection of bridesmaid dresses.

STANLEY KORSHAK
500 Crescent Court, Suite 100
Dallas, Texas 75201
214-871-3611
www.stanleykorshak.com
Celebrated full-service bridal salon—largest selection in the southwest.

THREAD DESIGN
65 East Oak Street # 2F
Chicago, IL 60611
312-475-0101
Visit www.threaddesign.com
for details of their two other
stores or a retailer near you.
Flirty, stylish, wear-again bridesmaid dresses.

VANESSA NOEL COUTURE
158 East 68th Street
New York, NY 10021
Call 212-906-0054 or visit
www.vanessanoel.com for
a retailer near you.
Stylish bridal heels, slides, pumps, and wedges.

PETER FOX
105 Thompson Street
New York, NY 10012
212-431-7426

www.peterfox.com
Comfortable, romantic, Italian satin wedding shoes.

VERA WANG
991 Madison Avenue
New York, NY 10021
Call 800-VEW-VERA or visit
www.verawang.com for
a retailer near you.
Exquisite gowns, bridesmaid dresses, shoes, and accessories.

WATTERS & WATTERS
4320 Spring Valley, #108
Dallas, TX 75244
Call 972-404-0143 or visit
www.watters.com for
a retailer near you.
Sophisticated bridesmaid dresses, plus elegant, well-priced wedding gowns.

CAKES

CAKE DIVAS
By appointment only;
call 310-399-2499
www.cakedivas.com
Upscale custom cakes, from classic elegance to over-the-top whimsy.

CHERYL KLEINMAN
448 Atlantic Avenue
Brooklyn, NY 11217
By appointment only;
call 718-237-2271

CONFETTI CAKES
102 West 87th Street
New York, NY 10024
By appointment only;
call 212-877-9580.
www.confetticakes.com

Sculptural, still-life designs.

JAN KISH LA PETITE FLEUR
P.O. Box 872
Columbus, OH 43085
By appointment; call 614-848-5855
www.jankishlapetitefleur.com
*Extraordinary cakes and sweet
accessories.*

MIKE'S AMAZING CAKES
14820 NE 31st Circle
Redmond, WA 98052
By appointment only;
call 425-869-2992
www.mikesamazingcakes.com
*Offbeat, unconventional,
whimsical cakes.*

RON BEN-ISRAEL
42 Greene Street
New York, NY 10013
By appointment only;
call 212-625-3369
www.weddingcakes.com
*Unique wedding cakes adorned
with exquisite sugar flowers.*

SWEET LADY JANE
8360 Melrose Avenue
Los Angeles, CA 90069
323-653-3771
www.sweetladyjane.com
*Fresh fruit cakes made
from the finest ingredients.*

SYLVIA WEINSTOCK
CAKES LTD.
273 Church Street
New York, NY 10013
By appointment only;
call 212-925-6698
www.sylviaweinstock.com
*Elaborate full-size and
miniature wedding cakes.*

CONFETTI

TOPS MALIBU
www.topsmalibu.com
*Butterfly-shaped paper
confetti, plus bubbles,
sparklers, and pennants.*

BRIDALINK
www.bridalink.com
*Pretty cardstock confetti
personalized with your
names or initials.*

JEAN M ESSENTIALS
Call 800-766-8595 or visit
www.jeanmessentials to
request a catalog.
*Bubbles, rice, lavender, and
birdseed, as well as wedding
favors.*

ROMANTIC FLOWERS
www.romanticflowers.com
*Silk rose petals, ribbons, and
paper for making cone-shaped
holders. Also candles and favors.*

CONFOTI
www.confoti.com
*Each piece of confetti
displays a photo.*

KEEPSAKE FAVORS
www.keepsakefavors.com
*Real freeze-dried rose petals.
Also place cards and table cards.*

FAVORS

BEAUCOUP
www.beau-coup.com
*Wedding and bridal shower
favors, including candles,
sachets, soaps, silver
keepsakes, and custom-*

designed cookies.

BELLATERRA
www.bellaterra.net
*Exquisite packaging and
invitation design as well as
well-priced flower seeds, candy
tins, matches, and CD covers.*

BEVERLY CLARK
Call 800-888-6866 or visit
www.beverlyclark.com for
a retailer near you.
*Cake boxes and other
presentation ideas.*

CRABTREE & EVELYN
Visit www.crabtree-evelyn.com for
a retailer near you.
*Their miniature soaps, bath
gels, and other toiletries are
perfect for bridal showers.*

CONFETTI
www.confetti-event.com
*Gorgeous boxes and custom-
monogrammed tags, plus hand-
dipped pretzel sticks and pink
French meringues.*

GODIVA
Visit www.godiva.com for
a retailer near you.
*Two- or four-chocolate
assortments in gold ballotins
with pretty ribbons and
decorative treatments.*

WEDDING THINGS
www.weddingthings.com
*Stylish keepsakes and
packaging, including affordable
monogrammed items.*

MY OWN LABELS
www.myownlabels.com
Personalized labels and hang-

*tags, plus Chinese take-out
boxes, tiny burlap bags, heart-
shaped tins, and other
presentation ideas.*

PEARL RIVER
www.pearlriver.com
*Colorful, stylish, and affordable
Chinese imports, from paper
decorations and lacquered
chopsticks to quirky candies and
satin pincushions.*

VOSGES HAUT-CHOCOLAT
520 North Michigan Avenue
Chicago, IL 60611
Call 888-301-9688 or visit
www.vosgeschocolate.com for
details of their other 3 stores or a
retailer near you.
*Chic chocolate treats, including
the Sophie bars, which are ideal
for bridal showers.*

INVITATIONS & STATIONERY

CARLSON CRAFT
Call 800-774-6848 or visit
www.carlsoncraft.com for a retailer
near you.
*Well-priced designs offering
traditional as well as
unconventional looks—whimsical
palettes, fonts, and shapes.*

WILLIAM ARTHUR
Visit www.williamarthur.com for a
retailer near you.
*Traditional, understated,
stationery with a contemporary
twist.*

CRANE'S
Visit www.crane.com for a retailer
near you.
Traditional, elegant invitations,

plus do-it-yourself wedding stationery, providing all the components you need to computer print your own invitations.

ARAK KANOFSKY STUDIOS

Call 610-599-1161 or visit www.arakkanofskystudios.com for a retailer near you.
Sumptuous custom-designed invitations featuring hand-painted details, exquisite calligraphy, and luxe ribbons and paper.

CARROT & STICK PRESS

6020A Adeline Street, Suite C
Oakland, CA 94608
510-595-5353
www.carrrotandstickpress.com
Charming, letterpress-printed place cards, stationery gifts, and custom-designed invitations.

PAPER GIRL

2158 Lawton Street
Fullerton, CA 92833
By appointment only; 714-446-9503
www.paper-girl.com
Exquisite, hip, handmade invitations.

SNOW & GRAHAM

Call 773-665-9000 or visit www.snowandgraham.com for a retailer near you.
Stylish, modern, minimalist designs. Excellent for bridal shower or bachelorette party invitations.

PULP INVITATIONS

Call 800-371-1796 or visit www.pulpinvitations.com for a retailer near you.
Stark, muted palette; smart save-the-date styles.

SOOLIP PAPERIE & PRESS

8646 Melrose Avenue
West Hollywood, CA 90069
Call 310-360-0545 or visit www.soolip.com for a retailer near you.
Custom letterpress and a wedding papers collection.

CHELSEA PAPER

www.chelseapaper.com
Chic online paperie representing numerous wedding invitation companies.

KATE'S PAPERIE

561 Broadway
New York, NY 10012
212-941-9816
www.katespaperie.com.
Representing distinguished invitation lines, plus print-them-yourself supplies, and gorgeous photo albums.

DECORATIVE ACCESSORIES/NOTIONS

M&J TRIMMINGS

www.mjtrim.com
Buy appliques, sequined flowers, ribbon, lace, rosettes, and rhinestones online.

KATE'S PAPERIE

140 W 57th St
New York, NY
212-459-0700
www.katespaperie.com
Ribbons, paper embellishments, boxes, and little bags.

MICHAEL'S

Visit www.michaels.com for your nearest store.
Craft supplies for favors, veils, silk flowers, and beads.

MIDORI

Visit www.midoriribbon.com for a retailer near you.
Luxe ribbons (velvet, taffeta, dupioni silk, and dotted organdy).

MOKUBA

55 West 39th Street
New York, NY 10018
212-869-8900
www.mokubany.com
43,000 ribbon styles and trims.

JO-ANN FABRIC

Visit www.joannfabric.com for your nearest store.
Well-priced fabrics, sewing supplies, and embellishments.

FLORAL & EVENT DESIGN

ARTFOOL

161 Allen Street
New York, NY 10002
212-253-2737
www.artfool.com
Creative, sophisticated, and unique event planning and floral design.

AVI ADLER

87 Luquer Street
Brooklyn, NY 11231
718-243-0804
www.aviadler.com
Whimsical, inventive, anything-but-typical event planning and wedding flowers.

BELLE FLEUR

134 Fifth Avenue
New York, NY 10011
212-254-8703
www.bellefleurny.com
Elegant, modern, wedding flowers.

GORDON MORRIS EVENT PLANNING & FLORAL DESIGN

7801 Melrose Avenue, #5
Los Angeles, CA 90046
323-653-0065
Unique, cutting-edge flower arrangements.

MARK'S GARDEN

13838 Ventura Boulevard
Sherman Oaks, CA 91423
818-906-1718
Lavish, exuberant, "L.A.-fabulous" designs.

TAKASHIMAYA

693 5th Avenue
New York, NY 10022
212-350-0111
Upscale boutique with an Eastern-influenced aesthetic. Glorious flowers, including large salmon-pink peonies (in season).

LOVE, LUCK & ANGELS

213-842-9952
www.loveluckandangels.com
Handles celebrity clients as well as budget-minded couples.

MUDD FLEURS

66 E Walton 1st Floor
Chicago, IL 60611
312-337-6883
Sophisticated weddings.

THE PERFECT PETAL
3615 W 32nd Ave
Denver, CO 80211
800-241-3418
Dramatic imported flowers and innovative arrangements.

LINENS & OTHER RENTALS

RUTH FISCHL
141 West 28th Street
New York, New York 10001
212-273-9710
www.ruthfischl.com
Fine linens, canopies, arches, and vases.

DURKIN AWNING
CORPORATION
90 Beaver Brook Road
Danbury, CT 06810
800-498-3028
Striped awnings and fancy white tents.

ROBERTA KARSCH-
RESOURCE ONE
818-343-3451
www.resourceone.info
Fine table linen, chair treatments, and table accessories; ships nationwide.

TAYLOR RENTAL
www.taylorrental.com
Everything for a wedding party, from candelabras to cotton candy machines.

SNYDER
843-766-3366
www.snydereventrentals.com
Ballroom chairs, shepherd hooks, tiki torches, and even dance floors.

GENERAL WEDDING RESOURCES

THE WEDDING LIBRARY
43 East 78th Street
New York, NY 10028
www.theweddinglibrary.com
A unique "research boutique" where brides can review the portfolios of the most exclusive, in-demand photographers, invitation companies, event organizers, florists, and caterers.

THE ASSOCIATION OF
BRIDAL CONSULTANTS
www.bridalassn.com
Where to find top-rated wedding coordinators in your area.

THE KNOT
www.theknot.com
The most comprehensive wedding website out there, with ideas, gowns, and vendors in your area to spare.

PICTURE CREDITS

Endpapers favor boxes from Confetti, striped ribbons from V V Rouleaux; **2** 28 Portland Place, London/gold-rimmed glasses, silver rose bowl and flatware all from Thomas Goode, crystal jug from William Yeoward Crystal, gold-rimmed table setting from Royal Worcester; **3 inset** candles from Price's Candles, silver beaded candle holder from V V Rouleaux; **4l** Skywood House, Middlesex designed by architect Graham Phillips/polka-dot ribbon from V V Rouleaux, silver-edged china from Royal Worcester; **4c** hand-made paper from Paperchase, wire mesh butterflies from Confetti; **4r** pressed glass plates and flatware from Marston & Langinger; **5** Skywood House, Middlesex designed by architect Graham Phillips; **6-7** Syon Lodge & Gardens, Isleworth, London; **6** floral china table setting from Richard Ginori, engraved goblet set from Evertrading, silver shallow vase from Kenneth Turner, chairs from Nordic Style; **7br** crystal wine glasses from William Yeoward Crystal, purple chiffon ribbon from V V Rouleaux; **8** (clockwise) wire-rimmed flower, miniature white beads, white silk and flower beaded ribbons, gold striped and polka-dot ribbons all from V V Rouleaux, mother of pearl dance card holder from Antique Designs Ltd., gold foil heart-shaped chocolate and sugared almonds from Rococo, faux white rose from John Lewis, white beads "2" from the Bead Shop, (center) white card and envelope from Paperchase, gold heart-shaped sparklers and paper bag with sequined flower from Confetti; **9** heart-shaped lavender ring cushion from Nordic Style; **10** embroidered cloth hanger from Cologne & Cotton, sequined flower ribbon and artificial flower bushel from V V Rouleaux, embroidered fabric from Lelievre; **11a** lamp and chair from Purves & Purves, stationery, notebooks and pens from Paperchase, white plastic file holders from Muji; **11b** (clockwise) braided pink ribbon with flowers (Braid JM 20E-02) from Jane Churchill, faux pink flower from Figaro Interiors, blue and white spotty fabric from Jane Churchill, beaded bag from Confetti, blue sequined flower from V V Rouleaux, picture/place card holder from Confetti, lilac stationery and blue flower strips from Paperchase, striped blue and white fabric with pink flowers (J26oF) from Jane Churchill; **12-13l** handmade stationery, notebooks and albums from Paperchase; **13r** multi-colored file holders from Rymans; **14-17** Skywood House, Middlesex designed by architect Graham Phillips; **14al** white silk dress from Monsoon; **14bl** John Rocha etched wine glasses from Waterford Crystal; **14r** tall tapered glass vase from Habitat, stainless steel and glass candle and menu holders from Menu A/S; **15** chairs from Purves & Purves; **16-17l** Jasper Conran plates available at Wedgwood, flatware from IKEA, damask napkins from Volga Linen; **17c** 3-tiered cake decorated with icing pearls designed by Eric at Savoir Design; **17r** heart-shaped mold ice cube tray from IKEA, glass ice bucket from John Lewis; **18-21** Syon Lodge & Gardens, Isleworth, London; **18** fold-up garden chairs from Habitat, flowered fabric with sylvan stripe on chairs from Jane Churchill; **19l** colored wine glass from Thomas Goode, Sia faux flowers from Figaro Interiors, spiral plate from Designers Guild; **19r** candy pink favor box from Paperchase, ribbon from V V Rouleaux, floral gold-rimmed plates from Royal Worcester; **20al** Chinese lanterns from IKEA; **20bl** gilt-edged cake stand from Kenneth Turner, favor boxes from Confetti; **21l** cream painted wire baskets from Fenwick; **21r** etched crystal goblets from Evertrading, spiral plates from Designers Guild, damask tablecloth from Antique Linen Company, pink and blue damask napkins from Thomas Goode; **22-25** 28 Portland Place, London; **22l** large pillar candles from Price's Candles; **23** silver rose bowl, cream napkins and gilt hoop napkin holders from Thomas Goode, gold-rimmed china from Royal Worcester, crystal pitcher from William Yeoward Crystal; **24** gold-rimmed glasses and flatware from Thomas Goode, gold and white china from Royal Worcester; **25l** silver rose bowl from Thomas Goode; **25c** gold and white china from Royal Worcester; **26al** favor boxes from Bomboniere, crystal wine glass and flower vase from William Yeoward Crystal; **26ar** fold-up garden chair from Habitat; **27** patterned china from Richard Ginori, crystal glassware from William Yeoward Crystal, flatware from Oka, wire beaded garland table decoration from V V Rouleaux, damask tablecloth from Antique Designs Ltd.; **28r** colored crystal wine glass from William Yeoward Crystal; **29** see p.27 for details; **30 & 31r** flower girl's dress designed by David Charles; **31l** white silk dress from Monsoon; **32l** vintage kimono apron top designed by K+K, pink and green flower fabric braid from Jane Churchill; **32c** white silk dress from Monsoon; **33** beaded bracelet from VV Rouleaux; **36-37** Skywood House, Middlesex designed by architect Graham Phillips; **36** 3-tiered cake decorated with icing pearls designed by Eric at Savoir Design, pink satin ribbon from V V Rouleaux; **37l-c** pink satin dress from House of Fraser; **39-40** 28 Portland Place, London; **40-41** all ribbons from V V Rouleaux, pearl-headed dressmaker's pins from John Lewis; **42c** patterned umbrella fabric from Lelievre; **42r** flower girl's dress from Monsoon, flowered handbag from Dickens & Jones; **43** braided fabric and pearl-headed dressmaker's pins from John Lewis; **44-45** patterned umbrella fabric from Lelievre, red and blue passementerie from Wemyss Houles, flowery braided pink ribbon sash (JM20E) from Jane Churchill; **45bc** flower girl's dress designed by David Charles; **46b** embroidered tray cloth from Antique Designs Ltd.; **47** embroidered table linen from the Irish Linen Company; **49r** heart-shaped wooden tray from Nordic Style; **50** Skywood House, Middlesex designed by architect Graham Phillips/etched goblets from Oka, flatware from IKEA; **51l** china from Royal Worcester, stemmed glasses from Habitat, flatware from IKEA; **51c** china from Richard Ginori; **51r** shot glasses from Habitat; **52** Skywood House, Middlesex designed by architect Graham Phillips/cups and saucers from Wedgwood, similar cylindrical flower vase available from IKEA and Habitat, blue-rimmed china from Royal Worcester, 4-tiered cake from Savoir Design; **53c** cream pot and wire-hooped plants from The Netherlands Flower Bulb Information Center; **53r** Jasper Conran plates available at Wedgwood, flatware from Glazebrook & Company, glassware from Stuart Crystal, cream and white pots and all plants from The Netherlands Flower Bulb Information Center; **55** 28 Portland Place, London; **55bl** flatware and pot from Christofle UK Ltd., crystal wine glass from Evertrading; **56-57** flower glass vase from Evertrading; **58l** 28 Portland Place, London; **58c, r & 59** Syon Lodge & Gardens, Isleworth, London; **59** chairs and cushions from Nordic Style; **60** white china from Royal Worcester, damask napkins from Antique Designs Ltd.; **61l** crystal glassware from Evertrading; **63r** Syon Lodge & Gardens, Isleworth, London; **64** flower girl's designed by David Charles, white painted wire basket from Fenwick; **65l** flower petal confetti from Confetti, white painted wire basket from Fenwick; **65r** white wicker basket from New Covent Garden Market; **66** flower petal confetti from Confetti; **67l** embroidered linen sachets and embroidered table linen from the Irish Linen Company; **68 inset** embroidered silk bags from Grange; **69** rustic wire basket from Fenwick, handmade paper from Paperchase, white fabric petals from Confetti, wire-edged ribbon from V V Rouleaux; **70-71l** cakes from Savoir Design, butterflies from C. Best at Nine Elms Market, Vauxhall; **71r** cake designed by Makiko Sakita at Confetti; **72** cake from Savoir Design, pearl-beaded braid and organza chiffon flower from V V Rouleaux, crystal champagne flutes from William Yeoward Crystal, china from Royal Worcester; **73ar-br** cakes from Savoir Design; **74l** embroidered linen coasters from the Irish Linen Company; **75** Skywood House, Middlesex designed by architect Graham Phillips/ 4-tiered cake decorated with icing pearls designed by Eric at Savoir Design; **76-77** cakes from Savoir Design/gold-striped ribbon and sequined butterflies from V V Rouleaux, gold-rimmed glassware from Thomas Goode; **78** heart-shaped cakes from Waitrose, pastry fork from Antique Designs Ltd., plate from Maryse Boxer (no longer in business); **79l** porcelain and chrome cake stand from Evertrading; **79r** silver mesh ribbon from V V Rouleaux, silver-rimmed china from Royal Worcester; **80a** glassware from William Yeoward Crystal, silver salt shell from Thomas Goode; **80b** etched glassware and glass flatware from Marston & Langinger; **81** glassware from William Yeoward Crystal; **82** condiments set from Thomas Goode, scalloped plates from Designers Guild, glass flatware from Nordic Style, etched glassware from Evertrading, sheer embroidered flower tablecloth and flower braid napkin holder from Jane Churchill; **83a** wire-beaded garland table decoration from V V Rouleaux, patterned china from Richard Ginori, flatware from Oka; **83bl** flatware from Nordic Style; **83br** patterned china from Richard Ginori, blue etched glass plate from IKEA; **84** gold star ribbon

from V V Rouleaux, engraved glass pear from William Yeoward Crystal, gold-rimmed china from Richard Ginori; **85l** ribbon from V V Rouleaux, cake knife from Antique Designs Ltd., china from Richard Ginori; **85r** embossed knife and fork set from Thomas Goode, silver-rimmed plates from Royal Worcester; **86** patterned china and silver coffee pot from Christofle; **87** patterned goblets from Oka; **87 inset** silver-rimmed plates from Royal Worcester, flatware from IKEA; **88** Syon Lodge & Gardens, Isleworth, London/chair and candlesticks from Nordic Style, pink plates from Richard Ginori, flatware from Robert Welch Studio, pink etched wine glasses from Evertrading; **89l** Stuart Crystal wine glasses from Waterford Crystal, martini glass from Thomas Goode; **90-91l** pressed-glass plates, cups & saucers, and crystal dish from Marston & Langinger; **91r** wire garland of tiny glass hearts from V V Rouleaux; **92-93** all ribbon and napkin holder decoration from V V Rouleaux; **94** napkins, gilt hoop, and pearl ring napkin holder from Thomas Goode; **95l** damask napkin and beaded tassel napkin holder from Thomas Goode, patterned plates from Christofle; **95ar** silver fretwork ring napkin holders from Grange, pewter bowl from Kenneth Turner; **95br** silver-rimmed china from Royal Worcester; **96** silk tassels with mink pompoms (made to hold keys) used as napkin holders from Robbie Spina; **97a** white porcelain rose napkin holder from Thomas Goode; **97b** scalloped plates from Designers Guild, flower braid napkin holder from Jane Churchill; **98** forks from IKEA; **99** embroidered napkins from Antique Designs Ltd.; **100** handmade paper from Paperchase; **101a** flatware from Thomas Goode, white bone china from Royal Copenhagen; **101bl** embroidered coaster from the Irish Linen Company; **101br** porcelain pagoda candle holder from Thomas Goode, patterned plate from Christofle; **102** polka-dot cups and saucers from Richard Ginori; **103** handmade cookies from Savoir Designs; **104** condiments, flatware, and place card holders from Thomas Goode, Stuart Crystal wine glasses from Waterford Crystal, china from Richard Ginori; **105l** champagne flutes from Evertrading; **106c** porcelain bunny place card holder from Herend Porcelain; **106r** tea set from Thomas Goode; **108** crystal cake stand from Baccarat, green glass balls from

Paperchase; **109** white miniature plant pot and silver tinned plant pot from the Netherlands Flower Bulb Information Center; **110** similar favor boxes from Confetti and Bomboniere; **111l** pink satin dress from House of Fraser, corrugated favor boxes from Bomboniere, cake stand from IKEA; **111r** gilt-edged cake stand from Evertrading, favor boxes from Confetti; **112l** boxes from Paperchase, faux flowers from Figaro Interiors; **112c** corrugated favor boxes from Bomboniere, ribbons from V V Rouleaux; **112r** colored etched wine glass from William Yeoward Crystal, ribbon from V V Rouleaux; **113** patterned plate from Designers Guild, ribbons from V V Rouleaux; **114** white bone china from Royal Copenhagen, embroidered handkerchief from the Irish Linen Company; **115a** Sandringham plate from Royal Worcester, floral handkerchief from the Irish Linen Company; **115b** china from Richard Ginori, handmade lace handkerchief from the Irish Linen Company; **116l** wire garland of tiny glass hearts from VV Rouleaux; **117** similar favor boxes from Confetti and Bomboniere, plate from Habitat; **118l & 119r** gold box from Paperchase, gold-rimmed china from Royal Worcester; **118r-119l** all plates and translucent onyx bowl from Thomas Goode; **119r** ribbon and silk flower from V V Rouleaux; **121** cake box from Bomboniere, fabric flower from V V Rouleaux; **122-124** truffles, bag of candies, and gold-wrapped chocolate hearts all from Rococo chocolates; **122r** martini glass from William Yeoward Crystal, plates from Wedgwood; **125** colored tissue paper from Paperchase; **126** candles from Price's Candles, silver beaded candle holder from V V Rouleaux; **127l** etched wine glass from Thomas Goode; **127r** flower and beaded garland candle holder from V V Rouleaux; **128ar** tray edged with glass beads and frosted glass votives from Fenwick, **128br** crystal candle holder from William Yeoward Crystal; **129** glass holders from Habitat, mirror from C. Best at Nine Elms Market, Vauxhall; **131l** glass Conran stand (now discontinued), glassware from Evertrading; **132ar** glass candle holders from Menu A/S; **133** glass lanterns from RK Alliston; **134** glass and chrome candle holders from Menu A/S; **135bl** fretwork lantern from Fenwick; **135br** white wire lantern from Fenwick; **141** Skywood House, Middlesex designed by architect Graham Phillips.

ACKNOWLEDGMENTS

My very special thanks go to the "team"—to my assistant, Paul Hopper, for creating such lovely bridal bouquets and wedding presents and for his constant cheerful support; to our brilliant and inspired photographer, the lovely Polly Wreford, for capturing romance in every picture; to our talented art director, Gabriella Le Grazie, for all her enthusiastic "Loverlys!" and for always joining in and helping us. My thanks, too, to Catherine Griffin, Pamela Daniels, and Matt Wrixon, for all their help and for posing as brides and groom; Claire Hector for finding such unusual locations; Chris Mills (Man on the Move) for safely transporting our wedding props from place to place; Biddy Akerman at Special Flower Projects for her romantic country flowers; Makiko Sakita at Confetti for lending us the beautiful wedding cake she made; Eric at Savoir Designs for creating the wedding cakes we wanted to eat but never could; Kate French at *Brides* magazine for all her invaluable help; a big thank you to my friend, Jill Koerner, for sewing for us at the eleventh hour; and my agent, Fiona Lindsay, at Limelight.

Also, I must thank all the stores who loaned us merchandise for photography—particularly Annabelle Lewis at V V Rouleaux, Thomas Goode, the staff at Confetti, Richard Ginori for lending so many beautiful sets of china, and Jenny at William Yeoward Crystal.

However, my extra-special thanks and appreciation go to three wonderful children— Hector, Caspar, and Celia Fraser—who made the ultimate sacrifice of missing bathtime, not doing their homework, and staying up late to model in our photographs.

Thank you all very much,

M.C.

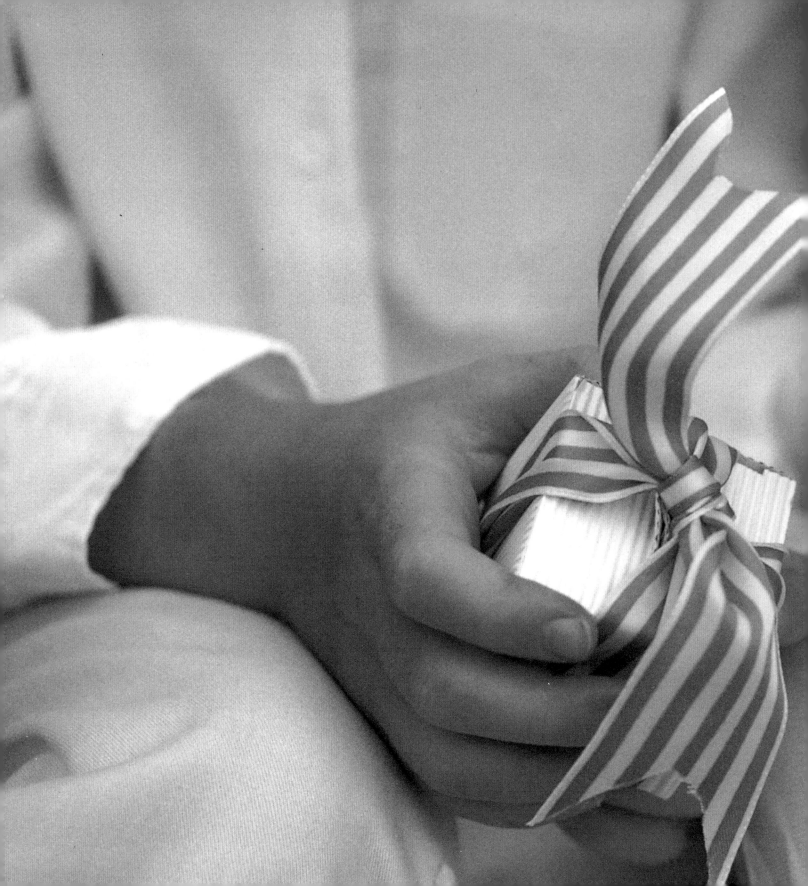